Brief Therapy Informed by the Single-Session Therapy Mindset

Brief Therapy Informed by the Single-Session Therapy Mindset

Windy Dryden, PhD

Onlinevents Publications

First edition published by Onlinevents Publications

Copyright (c) 2025 Windy Dryden and Onlinevents Publications

Windy Dryden
136 Montagu Mansions, London W1U 6LQ

Onlinevents Publications
38 Bates Street, Sheffield, S10 1NQ
www.onlinevents.co.uk
help@onlinevents.co.uk

The right of Windy Dryden and Onlinevents Publications to be
identified as the authors of this work has been asserted in accordance
with sections 77 and 78 of the Copyright Designs and Patents Act
1988.

A catalogue record of this book is
available from the British Library.

First edition 2025

ISBN: 978-1-914938-38-2

Contents

Preface

I became interested in single-session therapy in 2014 when I retired from my full-time position at Goldsmiths University of London. However, I had been doing single-session demonstrations of therapy in front of a physically present audience many years before that.[1]

In 2014, I decided to devote what remains of my working life to doing SST, training others in its practice and supervising people I had trained. I have helped many universities and charitable organisations that offer therapy to introduce single-session therapy services to the benefit of their clientele. These clients can now access, in a timely fashion, a therapy session focused on their stated wants. Such clients appreciate that they can be seen quickly and do not have to be placed on lengthy waiting lists, which had been the case hitherto.

My biggest regret has been that those services now known as 'NHS Talking Therapies for Anxiety and Depression'[2] have shown little interest in the single-session mode of therapy delivery. This is because they hold firm to a model where the first point of contact that a person has with such a service is an assessment session, these days usually over the telephone, the purpose of which is for the interviewer to decide which mode of therapy delivery is best suited to the assessed needs of the person applying for help. SST is based on a very different model, which explains why it is not a good fit for these NHS services. Thus, in SST, the client decides which service to access, and when they do access a service, whether they have chosen it or had it chosen for them, they often leave satisfied after their first visit. Ironically, NHS Talking Therapies Anxiety and Depression services only consider clients for outcome evaluation purposes

---

[1] Since Covid most such demonstrations occur in front of an online audience.
[2] These services used to be known an 'Improving Access to Psychological Therapies' (IAPT).

7

when they have made two points of contact with the service, thus excluding a sizeable number of people from being thus evaluated.

As I will discuss in the body of this book, the modal number of sessions clients have in therapy agencies throughout the world is '1', and a substantial number of these clients are satisfied with the help that they receive (Brown & Jones, 2005; Hoyt & Talmon, 2014; Young, 2018). SST does not say that everybody will be helped in a single session, and as we shall see, it certainly does not say that no further help is available to someone who wants it after the session. What it does offer is a timely therapy session for those that have been poorly served by our field. These people only want to attend very briefly and are either offered more help than they want or have to wait a very long time for help that someone else has judged is suited to them and where their voice is not adequately listened to. Due to my efforts in the UK and those of my international colleagues, SST is slowly beginning to be accepted as a valuable way of working therapeutically with many people.

I run monthly sessions on SST for Onlinevents and a certificate course in SST for its sister organisation, Temenos. In early 2023, John Wilson, who is centrally involved in both organisations, and I were discussing exploring what the single-session mindset could offer brief therapy, and this idea spurred me on to develop the ideas you will find in this book.

The book is divided into three parts. In Part 1, I will present a personal overview of brief therapy to introduce the book in Chapter 1. Then, in Chapter 2, I will outline key elements of the single-session therapy mindset, which informs my practice of brief therapy, which I will describe formally in Chapter 3. In Part 2, I present my work with Nicole, whom I saw for brief therapy for three sessions. The transcripts of the sessions I had with Nicole are included here, together with my commentary. Nicole provided a reflection based on a structured questionnaire for inclusion in this book, which appears after the transcripts. I close the book with some reflections and concluding remarks in Part 3.

The purpose of this book is not to show *the* way of practising brief therapy when it is informed by the single-session therapy mindset. Instead, it is to show that it is possible to bring a single-session mindset to brief therapy, and it demonstrates *one* way of doing so. As such, this book is best viewed as describing an approach to brief therapy that is experimental and very much a work in progress.

Windy Dryden
London & Eastbourne
February 2025

Part 1

Brief Therapy and
the Single-Session
Therapy Mindset

Preamble

In the first part of the book, in Chapter 1, I discuss salient aspects of brief therapy, especially as they provide a foundation for the approach to this mode of therapy delivery that I will present in Chapter 3. In Chapter 2, I outline key features of the single-session therapy (SST) mindset that usually informs what Talmon (1990) has referred to as planned SST (see also Hoyt, Rosenbaum & Talmon, 1992). In Chapter 3, I take both the salient aspects of brief therapy and the critical features of the single-session mindset and show how these can be combined in an approach that I call 'Brief Therapy Informed by the Single-Session Mindset'.

1

Brief Therapy

There have been many fine books published on brief therapy over the years, and it is not my intention to review them here (for example, see Garfield, 1998 and Bor, Gill, Miller & Parrott, 2004). In this opening chapter, I will discuss salient aspects of brief therapy as they are relevant to the approach to brief work that I will discuss more fully in Chapter 3.

What is Brief Therapy?

The first point to consider is what precisely brief therapy is. This is more challenging than it seems. For example, Steenbarger (2002: 349) stated that 'brief therapy ... is a generic label for any form of therapy in which *time*[3] is an explicit element in treatment planning'. Here, Steenbarger makes 'time' a central component of brief therapy. However, it is possible to make the number of sessions a central component of brief therapy. Table 1 (next page) looks at the interface of time and number of sessions in therapy.

- In Quadrant 1 of Table 1, the time period over which therapy takes place is short, and the number of sessions that the client has is few. I call this form of brief therapy: *Time- and Session-Limited Therapy*. In my view, most forms of brief therapy are forms of time- and session-limited therapy

---

[3] Italics added.

Table 1 Time and session numbers in therapy

		Time Period	
		Short	Long
Number of Sessions	Few	Quadrant 1 *Time- and Session-Limited Therapy*	Quadrant 2 *Session-Limited Therapy*
	Many	Quadrant 3 *Intensive, Time-Limited Therapy*	Quadrant 4 *Long-Term Therapy*

- In Quadrant 2 of Table 1, the time over which therapy takes place is long, but the number of sessions that the client has is few. I call this form of brief therapy: *Session-Limited Therapy*. An example is when the client and therapist agree to have a few sessions but spread these out over a long period of time. This arrangement would not be considered brief therapy from a time perspective, but it would be from the perspective of session number. The approach to brief therapy that I describe in Chapter 3 is an example of session-limited, brief therapy.

- In Quadrant 3 of Table 1, the time period over which therapy takes place is short, but the number of sessions that the client has is many. I call this form of brief therapy: *Intensive Time-Limited Therapy*. An example of this might be where the therapist and client meet every weekday for six weeks. From a time perspective, this might be considered a form of brief therapy, but from the perspective of session number, it would not be thus considered.

• In Quadrant 4 of Table 1, the therapist and client agree to meet over a long period of time and have many sessions in that period. Clearly, this is not brief therapy and would not be considered thus either from a time or session number perspective. I will not be considering therapy that takes place in this quadrant in this book.

How Many Sessions Constitute Brief Therapy?

There is no consensus in the field concerning *precisely* how many sessions of therapy brief therapy comprises. Leading authorities, Koss & Butcher (1986) consider 25 sessions as the upper limit for brief therapy.[4] Steenbarger (2002: 349) prefers a more nuanced position when he notes:

> There is no uniform dividing line between brief and nonbrief therapies. Instead, the range of interventions described as brief range [sic] from single session therapies in the strategic and solution-focused literature to episodes of 20 or more sessions in the short-term psychodynamic tradition. It is not at all unusual, for example, to find models of cognitive restructuring therapy that last for 12–15 sessions. This might be viewed as very brief treatment for a client with a personality disorder, but not one with an adjustment problem. Clearly, brevity is relative to the accustomed duration of treatment and the objectives undertaken by the therapist.

Whenever I encounter therapists who work in an agency where 'blocks' of therapy sessions are offered to clients, the

---

[4] Parry (2019) in the Introduction to her *Handbook of Brief Therapies* mentions an upper limit of 24 sessions.

modal number[5] in a 'block' is six sessions. When I ask why six rather than five or seven, the person I ask does not know. Given that six sessions are the number that most often describes brief work, I have chosen to use this number in the approach to brief therapy that I will describe in Chapter 3.

Most Therapy in Agencies is Brief

While some therapy agencies offer clients long-term therapy, many offer brief therapy. We know that the modal number of sessions clients have in agencies is '1', followed by '2', followed by '3', etc. (e.g., Brown & Jones, 2005; Young, 2018). We also know that in such agencies, 75% of all clients attend between one and five sessions. However, much psychotherapy training assumes clients will attend therapy far longer than most actually do. Given this, the challenge for organisations that train therapists is to adjust to the reality that, in general, clients are less interested in therapy than therapists are (Hoyt, Young & Rycroft, 2020).

Brief Therapy by Design or by Default

Brief therapy by design occurs when the therapist and client consent to meet for an agreed number of sessions at the outset, and when this number falls under the rubric of brief therapy. Brief therapy, by default, occurs when the therapist and client consent to meet for an agreed number of sessions at the outset, and when this number falls under the rubric of long-term therapy. In reality, the client only attends a number of sessions, and this number falls under the heading of brief therapy.

---

[5] The mode is the most frequently occurring number in a series.

Even when brief therapy is by design, the client may attend fewer sessions than agreed. I have integrated this point into the approach to brief therapy described in Chapter 3.

Selection Criteria

Garfield (1998) has written that most clients are suitable for brief therapy. However, he goes on to say that he would exclude people who have 'very serious disorders such as psychoses, so-called borderline disorders, addictions and the like'[6] (Garfield, 1998: 20). While some writers on brief psychodynamic therapy specify selection criteria for entry into such treatment (e.g. Sifneos, 1981), others do not. Thus, Wolberg (1965: 140) argues that 'The best strategy, in my opinion, is to assume that every patient, irrespective of diagnosis, will respond to short-term treatment unless he proves himself refractory to it.'

Some authors of brief therapy texts recommend a pre-therapy screening to determine if a client is suitable for this mode of therapy delivery. This was an approach taken by Safran & Segal (1990), who presented a brief, interpersonally oriented approach to cognitive therapy. Based on research, they found that those not suited to their approach were people who could not easily access their automatic thoughts, were not aware of or could not differentiate their emotions, did not accept personal responsibility for change, could not accept the cognitive conceptualisation of their problems, showed poor alliance potential both inside and outside sessions, had chronic rather than acute difficulties, did not have 'secure operations',[7] could not be focused in sessions and were generally pessimistic about therapy. As a result of their research, Safran, Segal, Vallis, Shaw & Samstag (1993) developed and validated a pre-therapy screening measure to determine a patient's suitability or non-suitability for

---

[6] It is a pity that Garfield did not explain what he meant by the phrase 'and the like' here.

[7] As demonstrated in the session by marked avoidance of discussing their difficulties.

their approach. This was done in the form of a one-hour, semi-structured interview.

By contrast, as we will see in Chapter 3, brief therapists who are informed by the single-session therapy mindset do not do this. Instead, they take the line adopted by Wolberg (1965), and once they have determined that the client has chosen to opt for brief therapy and understands what this means, they are happy to begin therapy at that point. If the client is not suitable for brief work at the end of the session, then this is discussed with the client and alternative therapy delivery modes are discussed.

Who Makes Decisions?

Two different positions can be discerned when we examine who makes decisions about and in brief therapy. The first is what I call the 'therapist/agency-centred' position. Here, the therapist is mainly in charge of deciding whether therapy should be initiated with a client and, if so, how many sessions and/or how much time should be provided for the work to be achieved. If the therapist is working in an agency offering brief therapy, the agency has often made these decisions. The individual practitioner who works for the agency implements them.

The second position might be referred to as 'client-centred'. Here, the client decides whether to access brief therapy and no matter how many sessions they agree to have with the therapist, they will often choose to have less than the agreed amount. In this position, the therapist is happy to go along with the client unless they have a good reason not to do so. On this point, both the client and therapist must give their informed consent to proceed.

The client and therapist can make joint decisions when they agree on a given point. When they disagree, the client will likely have the final say in 'client-centred' brief therapy and the therapist in 'therapist-centred' brief work. It is rare that therapy does not proceed when the client and therapist disagree unless such disagreement is profound.

Simple and Complex Pathways in Brief Therapy

Most approaches to brief therapy have what can be referred to as a simple pathway. The client is deemed suitable for brief therapy, a contract is made, and therapy begins and ends by agreement or when the client chooses to end earlier than previously agreed. The client is referred elsewhere if it proves they are deemed unsuitable for brief therapy, usually at the beginning of the process.

However, brief therapy can have a more complex pathway, as evidenced in the work of Elton Wilson (1996), who put forward what she called a 'time-conscious' approach to therapy. Her approach comprises a pathway based on three choice points. At each point, the therapist and client make the appropriate decision together. After an assessment/intake interview at which the client is deemed to be 'in crisis', 'visiting' (i.e., 'testing therapy) or 'willing to engage', the first choice point occurs where the client is seen in a 'holding' arrangement for between one and three sessions (which could be more than weekly) or seen for between four and six sessions having deemed to have made a 'mini-commitment'. The client then has a review (the second choice point) where the options are: (a) no further therapy, (b) continuation or (c) referral to a different mode of therapy delivery (e.g., group therapy). If the client continues, they make one of the following commitments: (a) a time-focused commitment (where the client is seen for 10–13 sessions in total with a firmly agreed end date); (b) a time-extended commitment where the client agrees to give four sessions notice of ending and has 12-plus sessions in total with an end in view rather than firmly agreed. In this commitment, several reviews are carried out; and (c) a time-expanded commitment where the client agrees to give two months' notice of ending, and the therapy can last up to four or five years with regular reviews occurring, and the ending date is mutually agreed upon. This last commitment is not 'brief therapy'. The options at the third choice point are: (a) no further therapy, (b) lateral transfer between commitments, and (c) referral to group therapy.

Contrast this level of complexity with the more straightforward approach to brief therapy outlined in Chapter 3.

The Initial Session in Brief Therapy

Much has been written on the first session in brief therapy (see Budman, Hoyt & Friedman, 1992). Most brief therapists regard the first session of brief therapy as an opportunity to get the therapy on the right foot by quickly establishing a good therapeutic alliance with the client and doing an initial assessment. On this point, Garfield (1998: 83–4) argues that

> The therapist will be interested in evaluating the patient in terms of several criteria. What type of problem or problems are presented by the patient? How serious are these problems? How interested or motivated is the patient in collaborating with the therapist in the necessary therapeutic work? What potential strengths and weaknesses does the patient seem to have? Are there particular stresses or crises in the patient's life that complicate the situation? Is brief therapy suitable for this patient,[8] and what are the chances for a truly positive outcome? Finally, the therapist should evaluate his own personal reaction to the patient and the prospect for a favourable therapeutic relationship.[9]

Having said this, Garfield (1998: 85) states, 'It is important to emphasise that the first therapy session *is* a therapy session and not just a session for assessment purposes. In this regard, he quotes Hoyt (1995: 288), who said, 'Brief therapists generally do

---

[8] As stated above, Garfield would exclude 'very serious disorders such as psychoses, so-called borderline disorders, addictions and the like'.

[9] Garfield argues here that if the therapist feels that they are not the best person to help the person, they should refer the client to a different therapist or mode of therapy delivery.

not consider assessment to be a separate process to be completed before treatment; rather, they see assessment and treatment as inextricably intertwined.'

As we will see in Chapter 3, when brief therapy is informed by single-session therapy, the work done in the initial session is guided by the client's goals for therapy and, in particular, their goals for that session. Any assessment that the therapist does is in the service of helping the client to achieve their session goals.

The Process of Brief Therapy

It is possible to take a process view of any form of therapy delivery, even single-session therapy (see Hoyt, 2018). Hoyt (1995) outlined five phases of brief therapy.

- *Pre-treatment phase.* Relevant factors here include what the client brings to brief therapy regarding understanding and hopes for the process and any changes they made between deciding to make an appointment to see the therapist and turning up for the appointment.

- *The beginning phase.*[10] Relevant factors here include engaging the client and developing a good working alliance with them, promoting positive but realistic expectations for change, setting goals (both therapy and session goals) and developing a working focus. Such a focus may be on helping the client to deal with a challenging event or situation, difficult emotions and symptoms or problematic behaviour. Therapists and clients must be active at the outset and throughout the process. Steenbarger (1992) refers to this as the 'engagement' phase.

- *The middle phase.* The main work in the middle phase is for the therapist to bring novelty into the work with the client

---

[10] See also the above section on the 'Initial Session in Brief Therapy'.

and, in doing so, to promote change. This is done by adopting a present-centred stance where clients can identify solutions or takeaways from the session and apply these to their everyday life. Later in this phase, the therapist will help the client generalise these takeaways to other salient aspects of their life. Steenbarger (1992) refers to this as the 'change and consolidation' phase.

- *The end phase.* The client may end the work as agreed with the therapist or earlier than agreed. The therapist should aim to help the client end the process so that their morale has been restored and with a sense that they have said everything they needed to say to the therapist and asked the therapist everything they needed to ask. Then they are unlikely to have any unfinished business later. In addition, the client should know that they can consult the therapist (or agency) in the future if necessary. If this is not possible, the client should leave with a clear plan concerning accessing future therapy services, if needed.

- *The follow-through phase.* Attempts should be made to discover what use the client made of brief therapy and to what extent they maintained any gains they made during therapy. Therapy agencies vary according to whether they follow up with clients and, if so, when they decide to do so. My own practice is to follow up with clients three months after our work has come to an end.

Outcome and Therapeutic Factors in Brief Therapy

Koss & Butcher (1986) have noted that outcomes are equivalent in brief and time-unlimited therapies, and Howard, Kopta, Krause & Orlinsky (1986) have documented that most changes occur early in therapy which in brief therapy can endure (Steenbarger, 1992). Steenbarger (1992) also reviewed research which indicated that despite the widespread view that brief therapy's positive effect is only with high-functioning clients, these effects occur across a wide range of client types and not just with those who are high functioning. His conclusion was that brief therapy is efficient as well as effective.

However, what accounts for clients' positive outcomes through brief therapy?

There have been many attempts to outline the factors that make for a good outcome in brief therapy. Parry (2019) cites work by Zarbo, Tasca, Cattafi & Compare (2016: 2), who proposed five therapist factors across modalities that were likely to lead to a good outcome in brief therapy; these were: 'the ability of the therapist to inspire hope and to provide an alternative and more plausible view of the self and the world; the ability to give patients a corrective emotional experience that helps them to remedy the traumatic influence of his previous life experiences; the therapeutic alliance; positive change expectations; and beneficial therapist qualities, such as attention, empathy and positive regard'.

In addition, Steenbarger (1992) mentions two client factors that are associated with a good outcome in brief therapy (i) good pre-therapy levels of client adjustment – where the better adjusted the client is before therapy, the better the outcome and (ii) client involvement in brief therapy, at emotional and behavioural levels, is associated with a positive outcome. The more actively involved the client is in brief therapy, the better the outcome.

In the following chapter, I will discuss aspects of the single-session mindset that I use to inform the approach to brief therapy that I detail in Chapter 3.

2

The Single-Session Therapy Mindset

Single-session therapy (SST) is defined as an intentional form of therapy delivery where the therapist and client contract to meet for a session of therapy and work together to help the client to achieve their stated wants from that session on the understanding that further help is available to the client on request.

While clients may seek different forms of help from the single-session therapist, the most frequent form of help is for emotional and/or behavioural problems with which the client has become stuck. Given this, I will discuss this form of help in this book.

While therapists from various therapeutic approaches can practise SST, they primarily use a broad range of therapeutic interventions underpinned by a set of beliefs about its practice known as the single-session mindset (Cannistrà, 2022). In this chapter, I will present and discuss the elements of this mindset and show in Chapter 3 how it can inform the practice of brief therapy.

One Session or More. Be Open to Both Possibilities

As the definition of single-session therapy demonstrates, the single-session therapist holds two seemingly different ideas simultaneously: to help the client leave the session with what they have come for, knowing that they can help if required. This dispels the myth that single-session therapist only sees their clients once.

It Is Possible to Conduct a Session Without Prior Knowledge of the Person

Therapists who practise long-term therapy are not used to beginning therapy without gaining much information from the client first. The same is true for therapists who practise brief therapy, although the latter will seek less information from the client than the former. By contrast, single-session therapists are happy to commence therapy without first knowing anything about the client. This practice has emerged from the experiences of therapists who work in 'open-access, enter now'[11] services where people would enter and see a therapist soon after, and the therapist would know little or nothing about the client in advance. Such lack of prior information about a client proved no impediment to helping them.

Start Therapy from the First Moment

Related to the point above, single-session therapists have in mind that they can start offering client therapy from the moment the session begins. They do not have to take a case history, thoroughly assess the client, or formulate their problems before initiating therapy. This frees them to do what the name 'single-session therapy' makes explicit – do therapy.

In some therapy agencies, therapists are mandated to do a risk assessment with every new client. If the agency offers SST, the therapist carries out a risk assessment and begins therapy after the assessment has been completed.

---

[11] These services are better known as 'walk-in' services but recent opinion is that this term is not welcoming to potential clients who are unable to walk.

View the Session as a Whole, Complete in Itself

The single-session therapist proceeds with the idea that they may never meet the client they are working with again. Given this, they view the session as one of a kind rather than the first of many and proceed accordingly. If they see the client again, they adopt the same view of the second session as the first. This is the case no matter how many times they may see the client.

Potentially Anyone Can Be Helped in a Single Session

Therapists with a conventional mindset towards therapy tend to think of indications and contra-indications for whichever mode of therapy delivery they offer. For these therapists, the idea that you can offer single-session therapy to anyone who seeks it, for example, in an 'open-access, enter now' service, is anathema. However, this is precisely what single-session therapists do. They argue that potentially anybody can be helped in a single session and thus offer it and evaluate with the client at the end of the session whether the client was helped and if they need further help. While SST therapists hold that anybody *can* be helped in a single session, they do not state that everybody *will* be helped in that session.

Focus on the Person, Not the Disorder

Whenever I give a presentation on single-session therapy, somebody asks me a question such as, 'Can you use single-session therapy with some who has "x" disorder?' My response is, 'What is the person's name, and what do they want to get from the session?' This response shows that a single-session therapist's focus is on the person and not on the disorder that the person has. Thus, ten people with 'x' disorder may want different things from SST, of which some can be achieved, while others realistically cannot.

The Client–Therapist Relationship Can Be Established Rapidly in SST

Another frequently asked question about SST concerns the therapeutic relationship between therapist and client. Can a good therapeutic alliance be achieved in SST in the time available, and how is this done? (See Dryden, 2022.) Research by Simon, Imel, Ludman & Steinfeld (2012) found that clients who derived benefit from a single session had a better working alliance with their therapists than clients who did not thus benefit. Thus, developing a good working alliance with a client is possible. My view about how best this can be done is as follows.

The therapist should first establish that the client has an accurate understanding of SST and helps them have realistic expectations concerning what they can achieve from the session. Then, the therapist helps the client to select a focus for the session and a session goal concerning this focus. Throughout this process, the therapist strives to understand the client's nominated[12] problem from the latter's perspective. Drawing on the client's internal and external resources and anything they have done in the past that was helpful, the therapist helps the client develop a solution to their nominated problem. They then encourage the client to rehearse this solution before helping them plan to implement it in their life. Finally, the therapist works to bring the session to a good conclusion for the client. This includes reminding the client that they can have more help if needed and how they can access this help.

---

[12] This refers to the problem that the client has decided to focus on in the session.

Be Transparent

Transparency on the therapist's part is a vital part of the single-session mindset. As the therapist may have little time with the client, they must share an accurate view of the nature of the therapy on which they are about to embark. The therapist is prepared to be transparent about (i) what SST is and what it is not; (ii) what probably can be achieved in SST and what probably cannot be achieved; (iii) what they can do as a therapist in SST and what they cannot do; and (iv) what forms of help are available to the client should they require more after the end of the session along with the possible waiting times for each type of help.

Single-Session Therapy Is Client Led

In Chapter 1, I discussed brief therapy and its salient features. One of its features is that the therapist mainly makes critical decisions such as: (a) Is the client suitable for brief therapy? If not, which form of therapy should I recommend to them? (b) How many sessions should I recommend to the client if they are suitable for therapy? By contrast, SST is client-led. This means the client decides to access SST if they think it might benefit them. If they choose to access SST, they decide what the focus and goal of the session should be. With the therapist's help, they decide what solution is best suited to dealing with their nominated problem and whether to access further help at the end of the session. The therapist makes their voice heard when the client chooses a direction that is, in the therapist's view, deleterious for them. The therapist's duty of care is to be clear about the possible risks of the client's chosen direction. Aside from this, the SST encourages the client to take the lead in what is, after all, their therapy.

The Client Decides How Much Therapy They Want

In SST, the therapist recognises that the client decides how many sessions to have and often opts to have one session. This is shown by the modal data that shows that the most frequently occurring number of sessions clients choose to have in therapy agencies is '1', followed by '2', followed by '3' etc. (as discussed in Chapter 1). If therapists could make clients attend as many sessions as they, the therapists, deemed advisable, these modal data would look very different. However, as Hoyt, Young & Rycroft (2020: 224) say, 'Clients are far less interested in psychotherapy than are therapists and prefer brief therapeutic encounters.' While there are exceptions to this statement, it does tally with the modal data.

Identify and Meet the Client's Preference for Being Helped

In SST, the most common form of help requested is a solution to an emotional or behavioural problem with which the client feels stuck. Failure to provide the client with this form of help under these circumstances will not lead to a good outcome from the session. Other than helping the client to solve an emotional/behavioural problem with which they feel stuck, there are other forms of help requested by clients. These include helping the client:

- To express their feelings about an issue;
- To talk about an issue while the client listens;
- To talk about whatever the person wishes to discuss without interruption from the therapist;
- To gain a greater understanding of an issue;
- To make a decision;
- To resolve a dilemma;

- By offering a professional opinion about an issue;
- By providing signposting assistance to other services.

The SST therapist has it in mind to provide the client with the requested service unless they have a good reason not to do so.

Providing the client with the requested form of help will increase the chances that there will be a good outcome from the session.

From the perspective of BTISSTM, I have found it useful to use Prochaska and DiClemente's six stage model of change[13] here to aid myself and my client to see where they are at with respect to the type of help that they are seeking. The important point is to work with where the client is at and to help them progress through contemplation to maintenance, maybe one session at a time (see Prochaska, Norcross and DiClemente, 2007).

Keep in Mind the Importance of Negotiating an End-of-Session Goal with the Client

In most forms of therapy, at the outset, the therapist asks the client what they would like to achieve from therapy. In SST, since there is a good chance that the therapist and client will only meet once, the single-session therapist is more likely to ask the client what they would like to achieve by the end of the session. However, since the client is likely to seek help for a specific emotional or behavioural problem, they may provide a goal related to their nominated problem. Consequently, I distinguish between a problem-related goal and a session goal. The achievement of the latter puts the client on the right path to achieving the former.

---

[13] The six stages are: pre-contemplation, contemplation, preparation, action, maintenance or relapse.

Keep in Mind the Importance of Co-Creating a Therapeutic Focus and Maintaining It Once It Has Been Created

Unless the client states that they want to use the session to talk about whatever they wish without interruption from the therapist,[14] the therapist must help the client to create a focus for the session. This is likely to centre on a problem that they have that they wish to solve, understand better or express their feelings about, a decision that they want to make or a dilemma that they wish to resolve. Once the focus has been co-created, it is, in my opinion, the therapist's task to ensure that it is maintained and also to check that the focus is still what the client wants to discuss as the session unfolds.

Unless the Client's Preference Is to the Contrary, an SST Therapy Session Requires a Structure

The SST therapist usually approaches the session with a process structure in mind. The exception to this is, as mentioned above, when the client wishes to use the session to talk about whatever they wish without interruption from the therapist. Besides this, the session has a very similar structure to that outlined in Chapter 1:

- The pre-treatment phase
- The beginning phase
- The middle phase
- The end phase
- The follow-through phase.[15]

---

[14] While this does happen in SST, it is not common.
[15] See Chapter 1 and Hoyt (1995).

Complex Problems Do Not Always Require Complex Solutions

Therapists steeped in a more conventional therapy mindset cannot understand how a client with complex and/or severe problems can benefit from SST. They argue that such clients need ongoing therapy to address such problems adequately. They may be correct. However, therapists' experiences working in 'open-access, enter now' services show that SST can be as beneficial for clients with complex problems as for clients with non-complex problems. These therapists tell us that clients with complex problems value non-complex solutions to these problems. Once they have implemented such solutions in their everyday lives, this can promote a virtuous cycle of change.

In addition, just because a person may have complex problems, it does not follow that if they seek SST, they will inevitably want help with one of their complex problems. They may be seeking help with a non-complex problem. As noted above, the SST therapist keeps in mind that they are dealing with an individual at a specific point in their life. Consequently, they should be mindful of the total picture of the client's problems and not be blinded by them.

Focus on What the Client Has Done Previously Concerning the Problem

When a person seeks help for an emotional or behavioural problem, they have likely made several attempts to deal with this problem before. Thus, they may have tried something that has made intuitive sense to them, they have tried something that a friend or relative has suggested, or they may have implemented strategies that they discovered in the wealth of self-help material that is widely available. They may even have sought therapy before for help with the problem. SST therapists are mindful of such possibilities and thus ask clients what they have done before to address the problem.

In doing so, they are particularly interested to learn what the client has done that has been helpful to them. In striving to understand these 'helpful' factors, the therapist must remember that what the client has found helpful may be unhelpful to them in the longer term. For example, a client with anxiety may say they have found reassurance helpful. However, on further exploration, the therapist discovers that this effect is short-lived and leads to further anxiety and increased reassurance-seeking. Once the therapist has identified helpful factors with no unwarranted longer-term unhelpful 'side-effects', they will use such information later in the session when helping the client to construct a solution to their nominated problem.

In addition, the therapist is minded to help the client identify past unhelpful attempts to deal with the problem. Once discovered, the therapist casts these aside while focusing on possible solutions with the client.

Focus on the Client's Internal Strengths and External Resources

SST therapists remember that they probably do not have the time to teach clients new skills that are not already in their repertoire. Indeed, they do not often have to do this because it is likely that clients already have these skills in their repertoire, but they do not realise this. Thus, SST therapists are minded to help clients look for their internal strengths and encourage them to bring these to the emotional/behavioural problem-solving process.

In addition, SST therapists are minded to assist clients in identifying external resources that may aid their problem-solving. Such external resources include people whom they know and trust who may offer suitable help and support as they implement what they have taken away from the session, organisations that may furnish suitable help and support and written material, audio recordings and applications ('apps') that cover relevant self-help material.

Think Pluralistically

Single-session therapy is best seen as an example of pluralistic practice. Consequently, SST therapists are likely to keep in mind critical pluralistic ideas as they approach working with clients:

- There is no absolute right way to understand clients' problems and solutions in SST – different viewpoints are helpful for different clients.
- There is no absolute right way of practising SST – different clients need different things, so SST therapists must have a broad practice repertoire.
- Following on from the above, different clients need different methods.
- It is best to take a 'both-and' perspective rather than an 'either/or' one.
- Acknowledge and celebrate clients' diversity and uniqueness.
- Clients lead the therapeutic process. Therapists facilitate clients in this respect (see above).
- Clients should ideally be involved fully throughout the SST process.
- Clients should ideally be understood in terms of their strengths and resources as well as their areas of struggle (see above).
- It is best to be open to multiple sources of knowledge on how to practise SST: including research, personal experience, and theory.

Be Solution Focused, if Relevant

I mentioned in the section above entitled, 'Identify and Meet the Client's Preference for Being Helped', that clients can seek different forms of help from SST, and it is essential that the therapist provides the requested help unless they have a good reason not to do so. I also mentioned that the most frequently requested help in brief therapy and SST is emotional/behavioural problem-solving. As such, I will concentrate on discussing solution-focused work in this book.

When the SST therapist thinks about co-creating a solution with the client for their nominated problem, they have in mind several sources from which they can draw in helping the client to identify such a solution. These involve identifying and utilising:

- The client's view of what might be a good solution to the issue
- The client's previously helpful attempts to solve the problem
- The client's internal strengths and external resources
- The opposite of the client's problem-maintenance factors
- The client's role model(s)
- The client's guiding principles and values
- Exceptions: When the problem might be expected to occur but didn't
- Instances of the client's problem-related goal occurring
- The client's experiences of solving the problem in a different area
- The therapist's view of what might be a good solution to the issue for the client

It is important to emphasise that while the SST therapist keeps these factors in mind while doing solution-focused work with a client, they draw from this list rather than using all of them.

Promote In-Session Practice of the Solution, if Feasible

Once the client has selected a solution to their nominated problem and is sure that they can integrate it into their life, the therapist keeps in mind the importance of helping them rehearse this first in the session, if possible. This is to help the client experience what it may be like to implement the solution in their life before committing themselves to use it. This is like them taking a new car for a test drive before deciding to buy it. It may be that the client may need to 'tweak' the solution or come to realise that it is not for them. In this case, the search for a better solution is resumed.

Results Are Mainly Achieved Outside the Session

The SST therapist keeps in mind the idea that the session that they will have with the client may well be the only one that they will have with the person (although it may not be), and as such, their main goal is to equip the client with a solution that they can implement in their life after the session has finished. They recognise that ordinarily the client will benefit most from the session if they implement what they have learned from the session in their everyday life. The exception is where the therapist helps the client to effect a positive reframe rendering their problem non-problematic. However, especially where the client's problem involves problematic habitual behaviour, any changes the client achieves will be done after the session.

Small May Be Beautiful

If the client can be helped to make a small change by the end of the session, which they commit to implementing once the session is over, then as mentioned earlier in the section entitled, 'Complex Problems Do Not Always Require Complex Solutions'. This can lead to the unfolding of a virtuous cycle of change. Thus, the therapist keeps in mind that in SST, small may be beautiful and encourages the client to adopt this view.

Help the Client Develop an Action Plan

Given that the client will probably need to implement their selected solution after the session has finished, the SST therapist will keep in mind that they will need to help them develop an action plan to facilitate such implementation. Doing so involves the client determining:

- *What* they have agreed to do (i.e., the aspects of the solution)
- *Why* they have agreed to do it (the purpose of implementing the solution)
- *When* they have agreed to implement the solution
- *Where* the solution is to be implemented
- *Who* the solution is to be implemented with
- *How often* is the solution to be implemented

In addition, the therapist is minded to help the client to identify any obstacles to them implementing this action plan encourages them to identify ways of responding to these obstacles if they occur and to take action to prevent them.

Have the Client Summarise the Session

Once the therapist has helped the client formulate an action plan to help them implement the solution in their everyday life, this indicates that the session is ending. When this occurs, the SST therapist has it in mind to ask the client to summarise the session. Usually, a therapist working from a conventional mindset might summarise the session for the client, but this would go against the principle of SST being essentially client-led. Asking the client to summarise the session encourages the client to stay active in the process. It underscores the view that the client will summarise what is essential for them to while the therapist is more likely to summarise what they, the therapist, think has been the stand-out issues. As the client is more likely to be influenced by their own summary rather than the therapist's, it makes sense for them to summarise the work. The therapist should suggest one or two additions to the client's summary, if they see fit. However, the client will decide whether or not to incorporate these points into their summary.

Ideally, the client's summary should include the work done on their nominated problem, the selected solution to this problem and how the client will implement this into their life.

Focus on the Client's Takeaway(s)

A client takeaway in therapy does 'exactly what it says on the tin'.[16] It is something that the client will take away from the session that is meaningful and can be put into practice. A takeaway should ideally include the solution the client has selected to address their nominated problem. Still, it may include one or two additional points that may have meaning for the client.

A takeaway is broader than a homework assignment which is a specific task that the client agrees to undertake at the end of one therapy session and reports on what happened when they carried out the task at the beginning of the next session. This is inappropriate in SST as the therapist does not know if they will see the person again.

Finally, the SST therapist must remember that the more the client tries to take away from the session, the less they will do so. In SST, more is less and less is more!

---

[16] In 1994, a British company called 'Ronseal' that manufactures wood stain, paint and preservatives developed a slogan to explain and demystify its products. It was 'Ronseal. It does exactly what it says on the tin'. This caught the public imagination and means something that is an exact description of what is being discussed.

Encourage Generalisation, Whenever Possible

The SST therapist has to hold a tension in their mind between helping the client focus on a specific example of their nominated problem and helping them to generalise their learning to other examples of the problem and related problems. Focusing too much on the specific means that the client will not be helped to generalise their learning, while too much focus on the general means that the client will not be helped to solve their nominated problem. Thus, the SST needs to be adept at seeing and using opportunities to do both.

End the Session Well so that the Client Leaves the Session with Their Morale Restored

Jerome Frank (1961) argued that while clients come to therapy with many different symptoms, they all tend to be in a state of demoralisation to a greater or lesser extent. Applying this to SST, the session's goal is, in part, to help the client restore their morale. Ending the session well plays an important part in doing this.

While ending the session, the SST therapist has the following points in mind:

- Ask the client if they have anything to ask the therapist about the focused issue they have not yet asked, but may wish they had asked once the session is over.
- Ask the client if there is anything that they want to tell the therapist about the focused issue that they have not yet mentioned but may wish they had mentioned once the session is over.
- Review with the client the options for accessing further help after they have had the chance to reflect on what they have learned from the session, digest this learning, implement it and see what happens. If they want more help after they done this, they will be clear about what options are open to them. These will include ending therapy at that point because the client has got what they have come for. All options must be

equally viable to ensure the client makes a choice uninfluenced by the therapist. All relevant options should be presented at the relevant time, along with the waiting times associated with each option.

If the client wants to book another session at the end of the first one, the therapist should explain why this is not a part of the SST offer. Clients need to get the most out of the first session (as described above) before deciding if that doing so was sufficient or if more help is needed.

Take Nothing for Granted

In a conventional therapy mindset, the therapist tends to take it for granted that if a person only attends one session of therapy, they did not find the session helpful. When this happens, the client is deemed to have 'dropped out' of treatment or terminated therapy 'prematurely'. However, in SST, clients frequently find the first session helpful and decide they require no further assistance.

When a given client chooses not to return after a first session, we do not know if they have or have not found the session helpful. We can only find this out by asking the person after the session. We can take nothing for granted on this point.

Thus, it can happen that single-session therapist may think that a given session with a client was helpful with the client fully engaged in the session. The therapist predicts that the client found it beneficial, but when the client feeds back, they say they got little from the session. Conversely, it can also happen that an SST therapist thinks a given session was unproductive in that they struggled to find a focus, and the client kept moving from one topic to the next. The therapist predicts that the client did not find the session helpful, but when the client feeds back, it is to say that they got a lot from the session.

As we say in single-session therapy, take nothing for granted.

In Table 2 (next page), I present a summary of the components of the single-session mindset discussed in this chapter.

Table 2 The single-session therapy mindset: A summary

- One session or more. Be open to both possibilities.
- It is possible to conduct a session without prior knowledge of the person.
- Start therapy from the first moment.
- View the session as a whole, complete in itself.
- Potentially anyone can be helped in a single session.
- Focus on the person, not the disorder.
- The client–therapist relationship can be established rapidly in SST.
- Be transparent.
- Single-session therapy is client led.
- The client decides how much therapy they want.
- Identify and meet the client's preference for being helped.
- Keep in mind the importance of negotiating an end-of-session goal with the client.
- Keep in mind the importance of co-creating a therapeutic focus and maintaining it once it has been created.
- Unless the client's preference is to the contrary, an SST therapy session requires a structure.
- Complex problems do not always require complex solutions.
- Focus on what the client has done before concerning the problem.
- Focus on the client's internal strengths and external resources.
- Think pluralistically.
- Be solution focused, if relevant.
- Promote in-session practice of the solution, if feasible.
- Results are mainly achieved outside the session.
- Small may be beautiful.
- Help the client develop an action plan.
- Have the client summarise the session.
- Focus on the client's takeaway(s).
- Encourage generalisation, whenever possible.
- End the session well so that the client leaves the session with their morale restored.
- Take nothing for granted.

In the next chapter, I will describe an approach to therapy informed by critical components of this mindset.

3

The Practice of Brief Therapy Informed by the Single-Session Therapy Mindset

Overview

In this chapter, I will outline and discuss an approach to brief therapy informed by the single-session mindset described in Chapter 2. I regard this approach technically as session-limited therapy, as detailed in Table 1 (presented in Chapter 1). However, I will refer to it in this book as brief therapy.

In outline, here are the essential elements of the approach.

- It comprises up to six sessions. The client can use the sessions at any interval over a six-month period.
- Clients do not have to use all six sessions. They can use as many or as few as they want. However, they may feel comforted knowing that all six sessions are available if needed.
- A client should not be in therapy with anyone else while seeing the therapist.
- Sessions will last *up to* 50 minutes. The session finishes when the work for the session has been done. The clock does not set the session length.
- The client is encouraged to prepare for every session.
- At the outset, the client will be asked to set a goal for therapy. They will also be asked at the beginning of each session for their goal for that session.
- The emphasis in each session will be on what the client can take away from the session, and they will be helped to implement these takeaways in their life.

- Whenever possible, the therapist will help the client generalise their learning from sessions to other relevant areas of their life.
- A follow-up will be carried out three months after the client ends therapy.

Bringing Open-Access to Brief Therapy

In Chapter 1, I described the critical elements of brief therapy, which is not informed by the single-session mindset. There, I discussed the work of brief therapy authors who think it is the therapist's role to determine whether or not to offer someone brief therapy (e.g. Garfield, 1998).

In this chapter, I will take a different tack on this issue by applying one key component of the single-session therapy (SST) mindset to brief therapy – it is open-access.

An open-access approach to therapy delivery is one where single-session therapy, in this case, is offered in what used to be called 'walk-in' therapy clinics which I now refer to as 'open-access', enter now clinics.[17] These clinics are open to anyone who wishes to have a therapy session whenever they choose to access it during the clinic's opening hours. The critical point is that nobody is turned away. Potential clients judge whether to access the service from information provided about the service online and on message boards in places like GP surgeries, outpatient hospital clinics and local mental health facilities. It may occasionally happen that a person has misunderstood the service on offer and enters looking for a form of help that the service does not provide. In this case, the person is received respectfully, given an opportunity to say what they want to say and then signposted to a different service. When such a person later requires suitable help from the service, they remember the welcome they previously received from the service and are encouraged to return.

---

[17] As I mentioned in Chapter 2, the term 'walk-in' is deemed not to be welcoming to those unable to walk.

Brief therapy informed by the single-session therapy mindset (BTISSTM) is also open-access. In my practice of BTISSTM, I make very clear what the service I offer is and then accept anyone who wants to access this service based on their understanding of it and their judgement that they may find it beneficial. Table 3 details my description of BTISSTM.

Table 3   What is brief therapy informed by a single-session therapy mindset?

Brief therapy informed by the single-session therapy mindset has the following features:

- You can have up to six sessions with me. You can use the sessions at any interval over a six-month period.
- You do not have to use all six sessions. You can use as many or as few as you want. However, you may feel comforted knowing that all six sessions are available to you if you need them.
- You should not be in therapy with anyone else while seeing me for brief therapy as described here.
- Therapy sessions will last *up to* 50 minutes. A session finishes when the work for the session has been done. The session length is not set by the clock.
- At the outset, I will ask you to set a goal for therapy. I will also ask you at the beginning of each session for your goal for that session.
- I will encourage you to prepare for every session.
- The emphasis in each session will be on what you can take away from the session, and I will help you to implement these takeaways in your life.
- Whenever possible, I will help you to generalise your learning from sessions to other relevant areas of your life.
- I will conduct a follow-up session with you three months after you have ended therapy sessions. This is to see how you are getting on and to get your feedback about the process of therapy.

The only way to know whether BTISSTM will benefit someone is to offer it and see if they benefit.

Help-Seeking Roles and BTISSTM

Based on the work of Seabury, Seabury & Garvin (2011), I distinguish between four help-seeking roles a person can occupy that have relevance to the approach to brief therapy that I outline in this book.

The Explorer Role

When a person occupies an explorer role, they have decided to seek help for their problems and have embarked on an exploration to discover what forms of help are available. When in an explorer role, the person may seek suggestions from their GP, relatives and friends or look online to see what help is available to them. However, in this role, the person has yet to contact a therapist or therapy agency.

The Enquirer Role

When a person occupies an enquirer role, they contact a therapist or therapy agency to ask questions that will help them decide whether or not to apply for help from that therapist or agency. A person may contact several therapists or agencies with queries concerning:

- What types of help are available, and what are the waiting times for such help.
- Specific aspects of a therapy approach which they are unclear about.
- The fees that are to be charged and if the therapist has a sliding scale of charges.

- Whether a therapist or agency accepts the private health insurance scheme that covers them. This will enable them to have their fees paid for by their insurance company.

Some therapists, aware that a person may be 'shopping around', offer brief, complimentary 'taster' sessions[18] to potential clients who seem to occupy the enquirer role. This is to encourage them to apply for help from that therapist after a favourable taster of what it is like to be a client of the therapist in question.

When I get a query about my approach to brief therapy, I check if they have read what I have said about this service on my website. If they have not, I refer them to this in the first instance and suggest that they contact me again if they have any specific questions.

The Applicant Role

When a person has done their research and has had all their questions answered, if they ask a therapist to take them on as a client, they then occupy the role of an applicant.

The Client Role

A person becomes a client after applying for help from a therapist and giving informed consent to proceed. Before they give their informed consent, the person should be informed of:

- The nature of brief therapy that is informed by the single session mindset[19]
- The therapist's confidentiality policy
- Any fees charged and how these should be paid
- The therapist's cancellation policy

---

[18] We know very little about such taster sessions, what happens in them and their 'success' in attracting clients.

[19] Henceforth referred to in this book as BTISSTM.

My practice is to ask the person to sign and date a contract, which clarifies my position on the above issues (see Appendix 1). When they do so, I consider them to be a client.

Helping the Client to Prepare for Their First Session of BTISSTM

Once a client has returned their signed brief therapy contract, the next stage is to make an appointment for their first and perhaps only session with me. In BTISSTM, my mindset is influenced by two principles: that the client may attend the agreed six sessions and that the session that we are having may well be their last.

Even though the approach to brief therapy expounded in this book lasts for up to six sessions, the literature on client attendance in therapy shows us that the modal number of therapy sessions clients have is '1' (see Chapter 1). This is why, although I have contracted with the client to have up to six sessions, I am aware that they may not use all of these sessions and may only decide to attend once. Hopefully, this is because they have got what they have come for, but it may also be that they have not found the session helpful and decided not to return.

While holding this duality in mind, I apply the single-session therapy mindset by encouraging the client to prepare for their first session of BTISSTM with me.

The Pre-Therapy Form

In Appendix 2, I have presented the pre-therapy form that I send clients before they have their first session of BTISSTM with me. As can be seen, the purpose of this form is to encourage the client to prepare themselves for their first (and perhaps only) session with me. I ask them to respond to the following questions:

- What issue or issues do you want to focus on in therapy?
- Why is the issue or issues significant?

- What do you want to achieve on this issue or issues by the end of therapy?
- How have you tried to deal with each issue up to this point?
- What strengths or inner resources could you draw upon while tackling the issue or issues?
- Who are the people in your life who can support you as you tackle the issue or issues?
- If you have nominated more than one issue above, which issue do you want to tackle first in therapy?
- What do you want to achieve by the end of our first (and perhaps only) session?

Finally, I ask the client to tell me anything they think I need to know about them that if I did not know then, from their perspective, I would not be able to help them.

As seen from this form, I indicate that the client has up to six sessions with me, but they can use as many or as few as they need – even one. This is what I mean by brief therapy being informed by the single-session therapy mindset.

The First (and Perhaps Only) Session in BTISSTM

At the outset, I find that asking the client if they have any questions about the therapy they are embarking on before we get down to business is beneficial. If they do have, I respond to them; if not, we can start. It is helpful to begin by asking the client if they have noticed any changes in the issue or issues for which they seek help, either from where they decided to seek help or after completing the pre-therapy form. If the client has noticed such changes, we can start with understanding them, especially if they relate to the issue they wish to focus on first, as stated on the pre-therapy form. If it relates to the other issue, I will ask the client which of the two issues they want to focus on in the session.

I will begin with whichever issue the client nominates. Initially, I aim to understand the issue in context from the client's perspective. This is often best done by working with a specific example of the client's issue. I will also utilise the client's form to discover what they want to achieve concerning the problem by the end of the session and by the end of therapy. I will connect the session goal with the end of therapy, problem-related goal if I can find a way of doing so.

In Search of a Solution: Ten Sources

After developing a keen understanding of the client's nominated issue in context, my next step is to help the client develop a solution. I encourage the client to draw from several sources as first listed in Chapter 2.

THE CLIENT'S VIEW OF WHAT MIGHT BE A GOOD SOLUTION TO THE ISSUE

It is likely that the client has their views about what might be a good solution to the issue. I need to discover what this is and what it is about the solution from the client's perspective that has therapeutic value. I will then encourage the client to incorporate these therapeutic elements into their selected solution.

THE CLIENT'S PREVIOUSLY HELPFUL ATTEMPTS TO SOLVE THE PROBLEM

Using the pre-therapy form as a reference, I will ask the client about their previous attempts at dealing with the nominated issue. In doing so, I will encourage them to capitalise on what they have done that was helpful and discard what was not beneficial.

THE CLIENT'S INTERNAL AND EXTERNAL RESOURCES

Again, using the form as a starting point, I will discuss with the client which of their inner resources they can bring to the table in finding a solution to the issue and which external resources they mentioned might also help in this respect.

THE OPPOSITE OF THE FACTORS THAT MAINTAIN THE ISSUE
I am particularly keen to help the client identify the strategies they thought would be helpful but which only served to maintain the problem unwittingly. In discovering these, I will be minded to put forward the opposite of these maintenance factors at an opportune moment so that the client can incorporate them into the solution.

USING ROLE MODELS
A role model is someone the client respects or looks up to and wishes to emulate in some way. The gap between the client and the role model must be such that the client believes they can emulate the role model's way of solving the problem. If the gap between the two is too big in the client's mind, then the person may think they will not be able to emulate the role model.

USING GUIDING PRINCIPLES
We all tend to have what may be termed 'guiding principles'. These tend to be value-based ideas or attitudes that encourage the client to act in value-based ways in salient aspects of their life. They tend to be pithy, memorable statements that people can bring to mind to help them, for example, deal with adversity. In the context of BTISSTM single-session therapy, they tend to support the implementation of the person's chosen solution.

EXCEPTIONS: WHEN THE PROBLEM DOES NOT OCCUR
Ratner, George & Iveson (2012: 106) note that 'It is impossible to behave with total consistency and however stuck in a problem pattern, there will always be exceptions, times when we do something other than the problem, something that with nurturing has the potential to become a solution.' As such, I might encourage the client to identify 'exceptions' to their nominated issue – times when the problem does not occur when it might be expected to occur. When we have found an exception, I will work with the client to discover which factor primarily accounted for

the exception and urge them to consider using this in developing their solution.

IDENTIFYING AND UTILISING INSTANCES OF THE CLIENT'S GOAL OCCURRING

Examining an instance of the client's goal occurring can yield critical information concerning what the client did to bring about this state of affairs. This information can then be utilised when the client comes to construct the solution

DRAWING FROM THE CLIENT'S EXPERIENCES OF SOLVING THE ISSUE IN A DIFFERENT AREA

When clients are in a problem mindset, they tend to forget about times when they may have solved the very problem for which they are currently seeking help, albeit in a different area and at a different time. Here, it is my responsibility to discover if this is the case and, if so, to help the client understand this and determine whether they can transfer this solution to the current nominated problem.

MY VIEW OF WHAT MIGHT BE A GOOD SOLUTION TO THE ISSUE FOR THE CLIENT

As an experienced therapist, I will likely have a view of the client's issue and what might constitute a good solution to the problem. However, I will typically wait to see what solution the client has come up with before offering my view on this issue. If I need to, I will offer my view on the issue by saying to the client something like, 'Are you interested in my take on what might be a possible solution to the problem?' It is unlikely that the client will say 'no' to this question, but the fact that I asked and they have said 'yes' means that they are more likely to listen to me than if I had not asked and just gone ahead and given my view.

Table 4 presents a summary of the ten points discussed above. Let me end this discussion by stating that I utilise only some of the ten sources when helping clients construct a solution to their issues. Instead, I have them in mind and draw from the salient points for a particular client.

Table 4 Sources to help the client construct a solution

- The client's view of what might be a good solution to the issue
- The client's previously helpful attempts to solve the problem
- The client's internal and external resources
- The opposite of the factors that maintain the issue
- Using role models
- Using guiding principles
- Exceptions: When the problem does not occur
- Identifying and utilising instances of the client's goal occurring
- Drawing from the client's experiences of solving the issue in a different area
- My view of what might be a good solution to the issue for the client

---

Types of Solution

In this section, I will briefly outline six solutions I routinely help people make in BTISSTM.

A REFRAMING SOLUTION

A reframing solution aims to help the client put an adversity-based problem into a constructive frame so that it is no longer a problem for the person.

AN ATTITUDE CHANGE SOLUTION

An attitude is an evaluative stance that a person takes towards an adversity. From my perspective, when a person has a problem with an adversity, this is likely because the person holds a rigid and extreme attitude towards the adversity. The solution to this issue involves the therapist helping the person develop an alternative flexible and non-extreme attitude towards the same adversity.

AN INFERENCE CHANGE SOLUTION
When clients make a change of inference, they are re-interpreting something more realistically.

A SOLUTION BASED ON A CHANGE IN THE PERSON'S RELATIONSHIP WITH THE PROBLEM
Here the person learns to accept or ride with the problem rather than fight against it.

A BEHAVIOURAL CHANGE SOLUTION
A solution that rests on a change is behaviour change based on the premise that when a person changes their behaviour, they invite a different response from another person with whom they have a problem. It also means that they are facing up to a situation rather than avoiding it.

A SITUATIONAL CHANGE SOLUTION
Occasionally, a client is best served if they change a toxic situation that they are in.

A COMBINATION OF SOLUTIONS
While it may be the case that a client requires a single solution to their problem (e.g., reframing), a combination of solutions is needed for another client.

Encouraging the Client to Rehearse the Solution

When you buy a new car, you will likely want to take the car out first to give it a test drive. As Sanjana Roy[20] has said, 'a person can only understand the features like safety, power of acceleration, comfort, noise of the car and smoothness of the car only after taking a test drive'. Similarly, before a client commits themself to implementing their newly constructed solution, it is suggested that they rehearse it in the session to see what it 'feels' like, to see if they can imagine themself executing it and to see if

---

[20]   https://www.linkedin.com/pulse/importance-test-drive-before-buying-car-sanjana-roy

any of the elements of the solution require medication or
replacing.

REHEARSAL METHODS

The main rehearsal methods employed in BTISSTM are role-
play, several imagery methods and chairwork.

Helping the Client to Implement the Solution

A good action plan shows the following:

- *Why* the client has decided to implement the solution
- *What* the client has agreed to do (i.e., the aspects of the
  solution)
- *When* the client has agreed to implement the solution
- *Where* the solution is to be implemented
- *Who* the solution is to be implemented with
- *How often* is the solution to be implemented

   Furthermore, it is important that the therapist ensures that the
client can readily integrate the solution and the plan to implement
it into their everyday life.

IDENTIFYING AND DEALING WITH OBSTACLES

It is helpful to encourage the client to stand back and consider the
obstacles they may face in putting into practice the solution that
they have committed to implementing. Once they have identified
likely obstacles, they should be helped to deal with them if they
do occur and take steps to prevent them from occurring, if
possible.

MONITORING THE ACTION PLAN

It is helpful if the client can record what they did when
implementing the solution. This can help motivate them and
provide important information if they should not get as much
from enacting the solution as they hoped.

End Well

It is a feature of single-session therapy that the therapist needs to bring the session with a client to a good conclusion because they do not know if they will see the person again. As the same is true with BTISSTM, I tend to end the session as I do in SST.

ASK THE CLIENT TO SUMMARISE THE SESSION

Asking the client to summarise the session marks the end of the first (and perhaps only) session of BTISSTM. Doing so keeps the client active and helps to ensure that they take away from the session what was salient to them rather than what was salient to the therapist. The latter is emphasised should the therapist summarise the session

ASK FOR THE CLIENT'S TAKEAWAYS FROM THE SESSION

A takeaway in therapy is a point that arose in the session that the client found meaningful. Takeaways should ideally include the solution the client has agreed to implement and one or two other meaningful points. If the solution is not included in the client's takeaways from the session, then this needs to be discussed with the client before the session ends.

AGREEMENT ON ACTION

It is helpful for the therapist and client to agree on what action the client will take after the session. Whether this is in the form of the action plan previously agreed, or a specific 'homework' assignment that the therapist and client have negotiated will depend on the individual situation and preferences of the client.

WAYS OF GENERALISING LEARNING

One difference between SST and BTISSTM is that in the latter, the client, at the outset, is asked to consider which issue or issues they want to deal with in therapy, whereas in SST, the focus is generally on one issue. Given this, in BTISSTM, I particularly look for ways of helping the client see links between the issues they wish to deal with and discover how they can generalise their learning from one issue to the others.

LAST MINUTE BUSINESS

Because it is vital to end sessions of BTISSTM well, the client should be asked if they want to say anything they have not yet said about the issue they wished they had said when thinking about it later. Also, they should be encouraged to ask anything about the issue that they have not asked about that they wish they had when again thinking about the session later.

FURTHER HELP

If you recall, in BTISSTM, as I describe it in this book, clients are offered up to six sessions which, should they choose to use them all, they can book at whatever interval they choose over a six-month period. While clients can have up to six sessions, they may choose to have as many or few as they decide to have, given, in part, what they have achieved previously.

For example, they may choose to have one session even though they can have six. Based on the SST mindset principle, the client decides how many therapy sessions to have. At the end of the session, the therapist reviews the possibilities concerning further help and does so as even-handedly as possible. The options are:

- For the client to end BTISSTM after the first session because they have got what they wanted from it or because they have not found it helpful and do not want to proceed.
- For the client to go away and process the work done in the session and put the negotiated solution into practice, and contact the therapist if and when they want another session.
- For the client to book another session at the end of the session.
- For the client to book two or more sessions as they see fit as long as they do not exceed the number of sessions (i.e., six sessions) or the agreed time period (i.e., six months.

Subsequent Sessions in BTISSTM

As noted earlier, in BTISSTM, the client and therapist agree to have six sessions over a six-month period. Having said this, the client can use as many or as few sessions as they wish at whatever interval they choose.

Preparing for Subsequent Sessions

Before each subsequent session, I ask the client to complete a form (see Appendix 3) on which they:

i.   Review what they have done to help themself on the issue we discussed in the previous session.
ii. Detail their progress since the previous session on each issue they wanted to discuss in therapy.
iii. State what they want to focus on in the coming session together with the goal for that session.

The First Session in BTISSTM is the Prototype for Subsequent Sessions

Subsequent sessions are conducted very much like the first session. Here is how subsequent sessions tend to unfold.

* The emphasis is on the issue that the client wants to focus on.
* The work is directed to the client's session goal.
* The therapist helps them understand the issue and why it is an issue for the client.
* The therapist helps the client to develop a solution to the issue if it is one that the client has not discussed before. If this is the case, the therapist encourages the client to draw from the ten solution sources presented in Table 4 earlier in this chapter. In addition, the therapist encourages the client to consider using what they found helpful in dealing with the issue(s) discussed in the previous sessions.

- If the issue is one that the client has discussed before, the emphasis is mainly on the strategies the client found helpful in addressing the issue, and these can be carried forward.
- If a new solution has been constructed, then the therapist encourages the client to rehearse it as before prior to committing to it
- Once the client has committed to a solution that they have rehearsed and can integrate into their life, the therapist, as before, helps them to develop an action plan to implement it. Also, obstacles to solution implementation are identified, and plans to deal with them are developed.
- The ending to subsequent sessions is similar to that in the first session. The client is asked to summarise the work and specify what they will do to address the issue discussed in the session. In addition, the client is asked to specify takeaways and generalisation is given increasing emphasis as therapy develops. Then, the client is given the opportunity to raise last-minute business on the issue under discussion, to which the therapist responds as appropriate.
- Finally, the client is given the same choice of how to proceed as in the first session. To recap, the options are:

  o For the client to end BTISSTM after the session they have just had because they have got what they wanted from the process or because they have not found the sessions helpful and do not want to proceed.
  o For the client to go away and process the work done in the session and put the negotiated solution into practice, and contact the therapist if and when they want another session.
  o For the client to book another session at the end of the session.
  o For the client to book two or more sessions as they see fit as long as they do not exceed the number of sessions (i.e., six sessions) or the agreed time period (i.e., six months).

The Therapist Monitors the Process in BTISSTM

As discussed above, every session of BTISSTM focuses on the issue that the client wants to nominate. However, the role of the therapist is to keep a macro view of the process, particularly as it relates to the following:

- The progress that the client is making on the issues that they indicated at the outset that they wanted to deal with in brief therapy. Progress is discussed with the client to get their view if therapy is proceeding as they hoped it would

- If the client is not making much progress on a particular issue, the therapist flags this for discussion with the client (see also Chapter 8 for an extended discussion of this issue).

- The therapist monitors the extent to which the client generalises their learning to other areas of their life. While the therapist should raise this for discussion, they need to do so that it does not come across as this is what the client 'should' be doing. Some clients are not interested in generalising their learning. They are satisfied as long as they are dealing with the issues they have sought help for, and the therapist should respect this.

- The therapist monitors for the presence of themes that may link to the issues for which the client seeks help. If a theme is found, the therapist should feel free to mention this to the client, and if it makes sense to them, the theme may drive the subsequent work. For example, a client may be seeking help for two issues which are linked by the theme of rejection. If it makes sense to this client to use this theme in therapy, the therapist may then focus the subsequent work on helping them deal with rejection constructively. Table 5 (next page) lists a schema I find helpful when looking for themes in the issues clients bring to BTISSTM. This schema lists the nine major emotions for which clients seek therapeutic help and their associated themes (i.e., what these emotions are typically about in thematic form).

Table 5   Inferential themes

Emotion	Inferential themes
Anxiety	Threat; danger
Depression	Loss; loss of value; failure; undeserved plight
Guilt	Moral violation (sin of commission and omission); hurting others
Unhealthy regret	Taking action in the past you wished you hadn't; failing to take action in the past you wished you had; facing uncertainty about taking action now or in the future in case you regret your decision later
Shame	Public disclosure of weakness; falling very short of one's ideal, negative judgement of self or of a reference group with which the person closely identifies by others
Hurt	Others treat you badly (and you consider that you do not deserve such treatment); others less invested in your relationship with them than you are
Unhealthy anger	Frustrated; transgressed against; ego attacked, disrespected
Unhealthy jealousy	Threat to present relationship posed by another person; facing uncertainty in relation to the aforementioned threat
Unhealthy envy	Others experience good fortune which you lack and covet

- As in every mode of therapy, there may be times when clients do not make expected progress and become stuck. The BTISSTM therapist is alert to this, brings it to the client's attention when it happens and facilitates a non-defensive, respectful discussion about what may be occurring for the client (see also Chapter 8 for an extended discussion of this issue).

Ending and Follow-up in BTISSTM

I hope you have seen by now that BTISSTM is client-led and very flexible regarding how many sessions clients choose to have and when they choose to have them. They are also free to end the process at any time they choose. Indeed, it may be the case that the therapist only knows that the client has ended therapy when the six-month period in which the client can have sessions has elapsed.

If the therapist knows that the client will end the process, they can discuss the client's experiences of BTISSTM in their final session. However, if the therapist only discovers that the client has ended when the six-month period has elapsed, they will only find out what has happened to the client when the follow-up takes place.

In my practice of BTISSTM, I usually suggest that the follow-up occurs three months after the client has ended therapy with me, whether after one session or after any number up to the maximum of six sessions. I prefer to carry out the follow-up by questionnaire which is found in Appendix 4. It is also possible to carry out a follow-up by telephone (see Appendix 5).

We have now reached the end of Part 1. In Part 2, I present transcripts of my sessions with Nicole together with my commentary.

Part 2

Nicole

Preamble

In this part of the book, I present my work with Nicole,[21] a 35-year-old counsellor who volunteered for BTISSTM by responding to a call for people interested in having BTISSTM with me that was put out by Onlinevents. Nicole signed a contract with Onlinevents and myself, which appears in Appendix 6.[22] Nicole received BTISSTM free of charge. As is typical in BTISSTM, I sought very little information from Nicole prior to seeing. However, I did send her a pre-therapy form (see Appendix 2). In this form, Nicole is invited to prepare for therapy by reflecting on which issue or issues she would like to discuss with me in therapy, what she wants to achieve concerning each issue by the end of therapy, what she has tried before in addressing this issue or issues, what internal and external resources she might draw on in addressing her nominated issue or issues, and any other information she thinks it is important for me to have before we begin. I present Nicole's pre-therapy form in Appendix 7. Chapters 4–6 present the transcripts of the three sessions Nicole decided to have with me accompanied by my commentary on my work in each session.

---

[21] Nicole wanted to be known by her first name and her husband was also happy to be known by his first name. All other names have been changed.

[22] To protect Nicole's privacy and anonymity, her *unsigned* contract appears in Appendix 6.

4

Session 1

Date: *24/07/23*
Time: *45 minutes 55 secs*

Windy: OK, Nicole, thank you for sending me through your pre-therapy form. What was the experience like for you filling that out?

         [Here I acknowledge receipt of Nicole's pre-therapy form – see Appendix 7 – and thank her for sending it to me. As discussed in Chapter 3, this form centres on what issues the client wants to discuss during therapy and gives the client an opportunity to set therapy-related goals, amongst other things.]

Nicole: I actually got quite emotional filling it out. I got quite teary. I'm quite an emotional person anyway.... Yeah, I just found it quite an emotional experience. I wasn't expecting that, but it happened.

Windy: What did you become emotional about that you weren't expecting to become emotional about?

Nicole: I think it was the first problem that I wanna talk about: like being like a child in an adult's world. I guess, when I was writing it, I was feeling it as well. So I kind of felt quite childlike and a bit, 'This is quite sad.' So I think that's what made me emotional.

[Nicole's emotional response tells me that one of her issues has great emotional relevance for her and shows that she is already emotionally engaged with therapy.]

Windy: You felt sad?

Nicole: Mmm [*yes*].

Windy: What did you feel sad about?

Nicole: ... [*Pause*] That I still feel like this, I think.

Windy: OK. We'll go into that. So, just to summarise from my perspective, you've got two major issues you want to deal with. One is a sense of what you've called, as a headline, Imposter Syndrome – feeling like a child in an adult's world. And the second one, in your words, overeating and weight gain, using food for comfort. Are they connected in any way from your perspective?

[Here, I summarise the two issues that Nicole wants to focus on in BTISSTM and I also ask if she sees a connection between the two]

Nicole: Yeah, I think so. I think they are, yeah.

Windy: In what way?

Nicole: ... [*Pause*] I guess there's a lot there that I could go into, but when I was younger ... it's odd looking back because I don't think I was an overweight child at all, but I felt like I was and I did use food as comfort ... and also, I guess, as discomfort. So I remember telling myself, 'Right, you can only eat one apple today and that's it.' ... Yeah, I kind of remember that day and just being really hungry all day. But also food was quite scarce at my mum's house. So my mum and my dad are separated, but at my dad's house it wasn't. So I would go to my dad's house every other weekend and we'd always have pudding after dinner and it would always be a Mars ice cream, and I just remember it tasting amazing. It was like the best thing in the world.... So I guess it's kind of connected in a way.

Windy: Can I just check with you, is it connected in a way so that when you feel distressed because of the imposter syndrome problem that's the time that you might turn to food for comfort? Is that the connection?

Nicole: No. I'll turn to food for comfort... with every emotion: happy, sad.

Windy: So it sounds like, although there may be some connections, it might be useful if we dealt with them separately.

[*Nicole's response to me suggests the importance of dealing with the two issues separately.*]

Nicole: Yeah, I guess so.

Windy: So you highlighted the fact that you wanted to begin with the imposter syndrome. Is that still correct?

Nicole: I think I would probably like to do the other one first, actually, because ... I had a couple of job interviews last week and I'm waiting for the result of those, and I'd quite like to talk about that another time with that when I know the result.

Windy: OK, right. That's the important bit, for us to be flexible. Although you said when you wrote that you wanted to start with the imposter syndrome first, you wanted to start with the other one, and that's, from my perspective, perfectly fine. So you said, in terms of what you wanted to achieve on this issue at the end of therapy, was that, on that one that you wanted to stop using food for comfort, and start using food for what?

[This shows the flexibility and client-led nature of BTISSTM. On Nicole's pre-therapy form, Nicole indicated that she wanted to start with the 'imposter syndrome' issue. In the session, however, she nominates the 'overeating' issue as the one she wishes to begin with. I go along with this.]

Nicole: … What it should be used for, I guess.

Windy: Which is what?

Nicole: Nutrition and to sustain life.

Windy: Nutrition and to sustain life.

Nicole: Yeah, to keep me alive. If I took food completely away, which wouldn't be a great thing, then I would inevitably, at some point, die.

Windy: So does that mean that two questions come to mind when you come up with those criteria: 'Is this food nutritious for me and will it save my life?'?

Nicole: … I don't think about that when I'm eating food.

Windy: I know you don't. Because that's what you seem to be saying: those are the two criteria for food. When I said to you, 'What do you want to start using food for?' you said, 'For nutritional purposes and to save my life.' That's why I asked the question: what would happen if you asked those questions before you ate anything?

Nicole: It sounds quite miserable, to be honest.

[In taking Nicole's statement about what she wants to use food for – nutrition and to sustain life and reflecting this back to her, she indicates how miserable that sounds]

Windy: Does it?

Nicole: Yeah.

Windy: So are we missing out something to do with food?

Nicole: Yeah, I think we are.

Windy: OK. What are we missing out?

Nicole: To enjoy it.

[Enjoying food is the missing ingredient.]

Windy: OK. So there are three criteria, then: 'Is it nutritious? Am I going to enjoy it? And will it save my life?' And, at the moment, you want to stop using food for comfort, right?

Nicole: Yeah.

Windy: Can I just ask you, if you're gonna stop using food for comfort, what are you going to be using for comfort instead?

Nicole: You see, this is the problem, because I've had quite a lot of therapy before, I've had CBT before twice about the food thing.

Windy: 'The food thing'.

Nicole: The food thing, yeah. And I remember being given a sheet and there was like a hundred different things that I could do besides going to food, and I ticked things that I enjoy doing – listening to music, singing to music, lighting a candle, having a bath.

Windy: Did they give you comfort?

Nicole: Yes.

Windy: You said you 'liked doing'.

Nicole: … Yeah, I guess so. Yeah, maybe it doesn't give me comfort…. I like doing those things but it doesn't soothe me.

Windy: Right. What soothes you?

               [*For Nicole, food represents not so much comfort as 'soothing'.*]

Nicole: … Food and… [*pause*] a hug from my fiancé.

Windy: A hug from your fiancé?

Nicole: Yeah.

Windy: Do you live with your fiancé?

Nicole: Yes.

Windy: OK. So what would happen if you felt, when you needed comfort, you reached out for a hug from your fiancé rather than – I don't know, we haven't talked about what kinds of foods you want to stop using.

[I wish that I had used 'soothing' rather than comfort here.]

Nicole: Chocolate mainly.

Windy: Chocolate, right. Any particular type of chocolate?

Nicole: Anything.

Windy: Anything with chocolate in it?

Nicole: Anything that's available, yeah.

Windy: So what would happen, do you think, if you thought, 'OK, I have a choice here: I can go for a chocolate-flavoured hug or a fiancé-flavoured hug'?

Nicole: … If the choices were in front of me … right now, I'd probably go for the chocolate. That's what I've been doing.

Windy: OK. So, even if the fiancé was available, you'd still go for the chocolate?

Nicole: Yeah. I think I see them as two separate things.

*[I am trying to link soothing from chocolate and
from her fiancé and put it as a choice point for her.
Interestingly she opts for chocolate.]*

Windy: OK. Tell me.

Nicole: So I see my fiancé as ... my partner and that's like
an emotional connection between us, and I see food
as a ... separate thing to that; it's not a part of my
relationship.... I don't know if I'm going off.

Windy: No. I'm just trying to understand that. So it sounds
like, to me, and you correct me if I'm wrong, that
somehow in your mind at the moment you haven't
found a way of – I'm not sure you've even thought
about it – recognising that you can have an
emotional connection with your fiancé AND he can
give you comfort.

Nicole: ... No, I think I can, but... *[pause]*, I don't know,
what I'm thinking is that I have a relationship with
food, with chocolate, and, if that stopped, would a
hug from my fiancé be enough to ... *[pause]* – I was
gonna say 'sacrifice' then, is it enough of a
sacrifice?

Windy: Well, the way you put it we could do an experiment.
We could test that out. Would you be willing to test
that out?

*[In retrospect, I could have explored the doubt that
reading this, seems to be implicit in Nicole's
wondering.]*

Nicole: Yeah.

[I could have asked Nicole for her degree of commitment to the experiment and if she had any doubts about carrying it out.]

Windy: Because I don't know the answer to that question. Do you know the answer to that question?

Nicole: No, I don't. I haven't tried it.

Windy: So, if we were to do that, how would it work from your perspective? Give me a realistic scenario that may be coming up that would involve you in a choice between chocolate and your fiancé? Does your fiancé have a name?

Nicole: Rob.

Windy: Choc or Rob?

Nicole: Yeah. So we're going away this afternoon for the week and there's gonna be lots of food around, lots of choices readily available as it's like a buffet. And I'm really worried about coming back on Friday just feeling even more big than I already feel. So there's gonna be lots of dessert options and usually I'd have two or three.

Windy: OK. And what do you want to do? What's your goal for this experiment we've got here?

Nicole. ... To not ... eat more than I need to.

Windy: And how much do you need to eat, dessert-wise?

Nicole: One.

Windy: One dessert?

Nicole: Yeah, if I'm still ... hungry or not full, which is rarely.

Windy: So are you saying that the other foods, that's not coming into the picture of overeating?

Nicole: Not really, no.

Windy: It's just the dessert, the chocolate?

Nicole: Yeah.

Windy: So we could say, and you correct me if I'm wrong, that chocolate and dessert is a vulnerability factor for you?

Nicole: ... [*Pause*] What do you mean by that?

Windy: You're vulnerable to eating it when you may not want to eat it.

Nicole: Yeah. I do want to eat it at all times.

Windy: Yeah, I know. I want hair at all times. So, in a way, we're also talking about your relationship, not just with food, but your relationship with your desires and how you manage your desires.

Nicole: I think that I don't have very good boundaries with food and with other things in my life. I feel like that comes into it quite a bit.

Windy: Well, you may well be right. We'll have a look at that. Do we need to have a look at that now before looking at the experiment or do you want to look at the experiment first?

[Here, I am asking the client to choose in which direction to go.]

Nicole: I think it's probably a part of it, so if we can look at it.

Windy: The boundaries?

Nicole: Yeah.

Windy: Can you think of a time, Nicole, that you can point to and say, 'Here was a time when I had good boundaries with desserts and chocolate'?

[Here I am looking to see if Nicole has had past experiences of having good boundaries so that we can use these going forwards.]

Nicole: Yes. So I've done probably every diet there is and I feel like I get to a point where I've put on an amount of weight and then I think, 'Right, that's enough. That's not good,' and then I'll go on a diet and I can stick to it – probably the least amount of time that I've stuck to it is like a day and then the most is a few months. But then I go back to my old ways.

Windy: Right, but tell me about the times when you were able to have a good boundary between you and dessert and chocolate.

Nicole: … I just sort of said no to myself. I don't think I even needed to say no, actually. I just didn't because I felt like my mindset switched from, 'You can do what you want, don't worry about it,' to… - I guess this links to the other thing: 'Right, you're a grownup, you don't need to eat all this chocolate.'

Windy: Right, OK. So, in a way, that's how you see the connection: there's you urging yourself to be a grownup as a way of being able to hold a boundary. Is that right?

Nicole: Yeah, I think so.

Windy: And that connects with the not feeling like a grownup in the other area of your life.

Nicole: Yeah.

Windy: And, when you aren't able to hold a good boundary with your food, how old do you feel then?

Nicole: … [*Long pause*] Ten.

Windy: Ten?

Nicole: Yeah. That's the first thing that came to mind.

Windy: Any special significance to the age ten?

Nicole: … [*Long pause*] Yeah, I guess it was quite a stressful time. My mum and dad broke up when I was six, but my mum met somebody else when I was eight or nine, and that was an abusive relationship.

Windy: What, between them?

Nicole: Yep.

Windy: But not with you?

Nicole: No.

Windy: But you were aware of this abusive relationship?

Nicole: Yeah.

Windy: And how did you comfort yourself?

Nicole: ... [*Long pause*] I don't know because my memory of when I was younger is really sketchy. I can't remember a lot, so I don't really know.

Windy: If you did know, what would it be?

Nicole: ... [*Pause*] Probably spending time with my sister. We were very close, so we ... had each other to look after.

Windy: And was that comforting for you?

Nicole: Yeah.

Windy: So you have got the experience where you can turn to another person for comfort. And what made it possible for you to turn to your sister for comfort?

[*Here, I am establishing that Nicole can turn to another person for comfort rather than to food.*]

Nicole: ... [*Pause*] Because we were having the same experience, maybe.

Windy: Right. So, if she was in a different household and you met, that would be difficult for you to reach out to her for comfort or would you still reach out to her for comfort?

Nicole: Right now?

Windy: No, then.

Nicole: Then.... Back then there was no way to reach out if we were in different households.

Windy: No. I'm just imagining that, if you didn't have the shared experience but you did actually meet quite regularly, I'm just asking you to imagine that, would you have still reached out to her for comfort?

Nicole: ... [*Pause*] Yeah, probably.

Windy: Why?

Nicole: She's my sister.

Windy: And?

Nicole: And we know each other inside out and we're basically the same person so we understand each other.

Windy: Right. Could you imagine saying the same thing about Rob?

Nicole: Yeah. Well, we're completely opposite people, but the way that our values and everything else is the same.

Windy: Yeah.

Nicole: And he understands me.

Windy: We'll come back to dessert and chocolate in a minute, but I think what you've done is not see the potential that Rob's got of giving you comfort, because, when we look at the connection between Rob and your sister, the important thing is not the shared experience but the quality of the relationship. And I'm wondering what would happen if you added to the quality of the relationship and said, 'Yes, I've got a good emotional connection with Rob AND I'm going to allow him to comfort me with hugs.' I wonder what would happen if you did that as part of the experiment that we're going to be constructing.

[*Having established that the link between seeking comfort and doing so from another person with whom she has a good relationship, I invite Nicole to see that she can seek such comfort from Rob, her partner.*]

Nicole: Yeah.... [*Pause*] Yeah, it would be interesting to find out, I guess.

Windy: OK. So, coming back to this weekend or this week and the dessert business, I wonder what would happen if you could disconnect the idea that only having one dessert is a mark of an adult. You don't have children?

Nicole: Yeah, I've got three children.

Windy: Have you got girls?

Nicole: I've got one girl and two boys.

Windy: So could you imagine only offering one dessert to your female child?

Nicole: ... Yes.

Windy: So you can imagine offering one dessert to a child?

Nicole: Yeah.

Windy: So it doesn't have to be connected to being an adult.

Nicole: ... No.

Windy: But you've connected it that way.

Nicole: Mmm [*yes*].... Having said that, my boys, I feel like they can have a dessert, but then 20 minutes later, if they'll ask for something else, I'll say yes.

Windy: Is that part of normal growing up for boys?

Nicole: Yeah, maybe.

Windy: What I'm saying is, it's almost like disconnecting and making connections. If you experimented with disconnecting the idea that only having one dessert is a mark of an adult because you do struggle with that as a self-image. So, if you say, 'Only an adult can have one, and I'm not an adult,' then you're going down a particular route, aren't you?

             [*If Nicole can disconnect the idea that having one dessert is the mark of an adult she can feel like a child and not turn to food for comfort but to her partner.*]

Nicole: Yeah.

Windy: And actually make a connection that you haven't made with Rob: 'That he can be somebody that can offer me comfort. I don't have to block it off.' He may not be as comfortable as an extra dessert. I don't know. But that's part of the experiment, isn't it?

Nicole: It is, yeah.

Windy: So can you imagine, as part of the experiment, to actually say to yourself, 'OK, I'm doing this experiment. I'm going to have one dessert because it's part of my criteria – enjoyment. I don't want to completely disconnect that and just have "Food is for sustaining life and nutrition." It's also enjoyable. But I'm going to have one dessert. If I need comfort, I'll ask Rob for a hug and see what happens.'

Nicole: Yeah.

Windy: Can you imagine doing that experiment?

Nicole: I can, yeah.

Windy: Can you see any obstacles to doing it?

Nicole: When I'm at work. Just talking about this week then, yeah, that's fine because I'm with him all week, but, when I'm at work and we're apart, then that doesn't work, 'cos we've got a vending machine that I often, frequently visit.

Windy: Right, OK. We can either take it a step at a time, which is that you've got this experiment to do, so you're gonna do it, and then we'll talk about how that went and then maybe we can incorporate anything from that to you dealing with the vending machine.

Nicole: Yeah.

Windy:　What would be in your best interests to do?

Nicole:　I'm off work for two weeks, so I don't have to think about that for a couple of weeks.

Windy:　So this is an experiment that could last for two weeks, if you choose to do it.

Nicole:　It is, yeah.

Windy:　Let's be clear from your perspective what you're gonna do as part of this experiment. So why don't you just summarise that.

Nicole:　Yeah. So on holiday this week at the buffet, when I'm looking at the desserts, I'll choose one and then, if I'm still not satisfied after that one and I want more, which is probably likely, I will give my fiancé, Rob, a hug and just have a little cuddle for a bit and see how that goes.

Windy:　Right. So how would you feel if it wasn't part of the experiment and Rob wasn't around and you had one dessert and you wanted another one? How do you think you'd feel if you didn't act on that want?

Nicole:　… [*Long pause*] Like a grownup. I've made a grownup decision.

Windy:　So the immediate response is what you'd gained by that: 'I've said no to the second dessert, this is a mark of an adult'?

Nicole:　Mmm [*yes*].

Windy: OK, that's good. What about what you'd lose? How would you feel about what you'd lose?

Nicole: … Enjoyment and comfort.

Windy: Enjoyment and comfort.

Nicole: Yeah, in the moment.

Windy: In the moment.

Nicole: Yeah.

Windy: Now, what do you think your stance is towards enjoyment and comfort in the moment? When I say stance, it could be an attitude or your viewpoint.

Nicole: … [*Pause*] I like to think that I live in the moment, but then I'm quite an anxious person, so I look at stuff in the future quite a lot.

Windy: No, I'm talking about at that moment you've had a dessert, there's a possibility of the second one, you've said no to it temporarily. Part of you is saying, 'Hey, this is a sign of an adult here.' The other part of it is not getting what you want.

[*I have in mind that I need to help Nicole deal with the feelings of not getting what she wants in the moment when she does not eat the desired food.*]

Nicole: Yeah.

Windy: I'm just saying how do you feel about not getting what you want: that enjoyment, that comfort in the moment? You're not going for enjoyment and comfort in the moment. If you don't do that, how do you feel?

Nicole: … [*Long pause*] Upset.

Windy: What kind of upset?

Nicole: Like I'm missing out on something…. [*Pause*] Like there's nothing to look forward to.

Windy: OK. And that upset, I'm not quite sure what feeling that is. Upset can come in different flavours.

Nicole: Yeah. I guess what I said just then: like I don't have anything to look forward to.

Windy: 'So I don't have anything to look forward to and I'm missing out on something.'

Nicole: Yeah.

Windy: To me that sounds like separate things. I don't know whether that is to you or for you it's one. But are they separate experiences?

Nicole: It is separate, yeah.

Windy: So which one do you want to start with first?

Nicole: Got nothing to look forward to.

Windy: OK. So let's have a look at that. How old are you?

Nicole: 35.

Windy: So 35. I'm going to look into my crystal ball and I'm going to look at 36. There you are at 36 – no, nothing to look forward to. 37 – nothing. 45 – nope. 60 – not a thing.

Nicole: Yeah, as soon as I said it, I realised how silly that sounds and it's not true.

Windy: Right, but don't say it's silly because you're in danger of then saying, 'I shouldn't think this.' Then you actually go down a different rabbit hole. Why don't you just accept that that is a thought that you have and that it's just a thought and you can investigate it? You can stand back and ask yourself what?

Nicole: Is that true.

Windy: Right. And is it?

Nicole: No.

Windy: No. I mean, what kind of things do you look forward to in life?

Nicole: Spending time with my children. A lot of parents don't look forward to the summer holidays, but I love it because I love spending time with them – going to the cinema, spending time with my other half.

Windy: So can you imagine then having that thought, 'I've got nothing to look forward to. If I don't have this second dessert, I've got nothing to look forward to. Wait a minute, that's a kind of thought that I tend to have, but it's not true. I've got my kids to look forward to'? Do you enjoy looking forward to Rob?

Nicole: Yeah.

Windy: 'I've got Rob to look forward to', right?

Nicole: Yeah.

Windy: Now, what do you think would happen with that thought, 'I've got nothing to look forward to', if you responded to it in those ways?

Nicole: As in challenging it?

Windy: Examining it. I wouldn't say challenging it. Examining it.

Nicole: ... Yeah.... I guess that's the good thing about this is digging in and what am I actually thinking and feeling.

Windy: Yeah.

Nicole: And I hadn't thought about, because that is what I think: 'Well, I've got nothing to look forward to.'

Windy: So you might as well.

Nicole: Yeah. So, yeah, I can definitely see myself looking at it.

Windy: Could that be a part of the experiment, right?

            [*I am suggesting that Nicole incorporate examining and responding to the thought, 'I have nothing to look forward to' as part of the experiment we have been discussing.*]

Nicole: Yeah. Two parts now.

Windy: Well, it's the same experiment: we're just giving you a bit more of an oomph; we're giving it a proper chance to really test it out.

Nicole: Yeah.

Windy: Let's have a look at the other thought or feeling or both: 'I'm missing out.'

Nicole: Yeah.

Windy: What are you missing out on?

Nicole: The enjoyment and the way it tastes and the comfort.

Windy: Yeah, OK, and you would be missing out on that. And how do you feel about missing out?

Nicole: That sounds quite childlike, doesn't it, that I'm missing out? I can't do something so I'm missing out on it.

Windy: Well, again, if you were to view it as an initial thought, because that's what we're talking about, isn't it? It's an initial thought: 'I'm missing out.' Well, actually, it's true. We can't argue about that. You would be missing out on that extra dessert.

Nicole: Yeah.

Windy: The way I see it, and I don't know if you'd be interested in my take on it, that is you have a choice of saying, 'I mustn't miss out. It's unbearable to miss out,' or, 'I don't like missing out but that doesn't mean that it's something that I mustn't experience. It's worth bearing because it will lead to something that I want.'

[*I wish I had asked Nicole more directly if she would have liked my 'take' on the issue and waited for her affirmative response before offering my view.*]

Nicole: Mmm [*yes*] … [*pause*] yeah. I guess the thing is I'm not really missing out because I can have it the next day.

Windy: Yeah. But, even if you are missing out, I think, in a way, although you're right, you're not missing out, but actually you are missing out in the moment. So what I'm saying is would it be useful for you to equip yourself with a way of dealing with that missing out sense that will actually serve you towards meeting your goal, which is to stop using food for comfort?

[*Here, I am encouraging Nicole to recognise that in the moment she is missing out on the dessert but that she can bear missing out because it is worth it to her to do so.*]

Nicole: Yeah. I don't know what that would be. I guess just examining the thought again.

Windy: Yeah, standing back and saying, 'Look, I've got a choice: I mustn't miss out, obviously I can – is it worth bearing or isn't it?' And is it worth bearing?

Nicole: … It is because it's temporary.

Windy: Yeah. We're not saying, 'This is the last dessert in the universe. You miss out on this, Nicole, and that is it.'

Nicole: Yeah, forever.

Windy: Forever.

Nicole: Yeah. It's a temporary thing.

Windy: Yeah, and is it worth bearing because it's temporary?

Nicole: Yeah.

Windy: Are you willing to bear it?

Nicole: I'm willing to give it a good go.

Windy: What does that mean, 'give it a good go'?

Nicole: Because I feel like … I've tried so many different things … and each time I'm like, 'Right, this is it.'

Windy: It's all part of the experiment, you see.

Nicole: Yeah. And I feel like, if I commit myself 100% and I fail, then I'm going to be really upset with myself. So, if I say I'm going to give it a go, that's not.

Windy: Yeah. I see it a little differently. I think you can commit yourself to doing it 100%. If you don't do it then we have more information that we didn't have.

Nicole: Yeah.

Windy: In a way, you're getting feedback.

Nicole: Yeah. I think, because I've failed so many times, I don't trust myself, because I want to believe and I feel like I can do this.

Windy: Sure. Has the focus that we're talking about now, which is whether you can bear missing out in the moment or not, has that been a feature of any therapy that you've had before?

Nicole: Yeah, it has, sitting with the feeling, which I hate ... that saying and I hate doing it.

Windy: Right.

Nicole: Because who wants to feel uncomfortable? Nobody. But it's a part of life, so just get on with it. But I don't want to, obviously, because otherwise I wouldn't use food for comfort.

Windy: Right. So what's gonna be different about this particular way of looking at it for you?

Nicole: Because I'm the biggest that I've ever been and I know that I'm just going to continue along this path.

Windy: No, I meant looking at it in terms of being willing to bear it?

Nicole: What's different this time?

Windy: Yeah. In the sense that is it the same as sitting with the feeling or is it different when we talk about being willing and committed to bearing the missing out?

Nicole: Yeah.

Windy: Is there a difference for you?

Nicole: It feels like there's other ... elements that I can bring in, like going to Rob or something like that. It's not a part on its own. There's different ... features to it that I can use, so it's not like a standalone, because I think if it was then I'm not sure how I would be able to just sit with it.

[*From Nicole's perspective, the twofold nature of the experiment is important.*]

Windy: You mean if it wasn't linked to the other part of the experiment, which is going to Rob for some comfort and to see what happens then. So it's linked to that.

Nicole: Yeah.

Windy: Again, we can have a look at that experiment. Just one other thing about that, I'm not talking about this list of a hundred things that you can do, which I think you confuse with, 'Oh, I like that' or, 'I don't like that'. But I just wonder if you've ever had the experience of comforting yourself in ways that didn't involve food, because there's a sense of, when you talk about hug and your sister, I have a sense of a more physical part of it, and I was wondering if there was anything, for you, that you've ever experienced or could experience that might give you a sense of comfort that had a physical sense that didn't involve food.

Nicole: ... [*Long pause*] I don't think so.... I'm thinking of things that I do that aren't great to comfort me instead. But I don't know that there's something else. I mean, my children, hugging them as well.

Windy: Yeah. That's important.

Nicole: Yeah.

Windy: There are a couple of things that come to mind which I could share if you're interested to hear.

Nicole: Yeah.

Windy: And I'd be interested to hear what you've got to say. There's something from the tapping therapies that involves somebody tapping this, and that can be quite calming and soothing. And have you heard of havening?

Nicole: No.

Windy: Well, havening is where you hug yourself like that.

Nicole: Yeah.

Windy: Do you wanna just try that out, see how it feels?

Nicole: … It feels quite comforting. Yeah, it's nice.

Windy: So, in a way, to add to your repertoire of comfort, there's a physicality that I think is missing, and maybe you could experiment with doing the havening and the tapping, see how it goes.

                [Here, I have suggested two things that Nicole can use that incorporate a physical aspect to self-comfort which seems important.]

Nicole: Yeah.

Windy: So, we've got alternatives to food for comfort, haven't we? We've got hugging from Rob, hugging from your kids, self-hugging with havening and tapping, as well as building up your being able to bear the discomfort involved with missing out, and looking and standing back and saying, 'Well, actually, it's not true that I won't have anything to look forward to.'

Nicole: Yeah, so I've got quite a lot in my armoury.

Windy: Yeah, and I invite you to carry out that experiment. I think you've got a great opportunity to do that over the next couple of weeks.

Nicole: Yeah, I have.

Windy: So why don't you summarise what we've done today?

[*As in single-session therapy, in BTISSTM, I encourage Nicole to provide a summary rather than providing one for her.*]

Nicole: So we've looked at ... how I use food for comfort and it feels like we've digged down into it and what I'm really thinking and feeling and what I can do as an alternative to ... reaching for food, and those alternatives are: go to Rob/my kids for hugs; I think I'd like to add also that I can call my sister – I always like having a chat with her; giving myself a hug; the tapping technique and looking at what I'm thinking as actually true when it's not. I do have stuff to look forward to and it doesn't have to be immediate.

Windy: Yeah, and the sense of being able to bear missing out in the moment.

Nicole: Yeah.

Windy: So that's gonna be your takeaway as well?

Nicole: Yeah.

Windy: We're talking about food – a takeaway. Is there anything that we talked about or that I did that you found unhelpful today? I do invite you to be as honest as you can because that will help me to calibrate the therapy with you. So I'm going to be asking you routinely anything I did that was unhelpful, anything that I did hat was helpful. So that will be useful for me to hear and calibrate.

Nicole: Not that I can think of in this moment, but, if something comes up when I've reflected on the session and what we've spoken about, then I'll let you know if anything does come up.

Windy: Please. And anything that was helpful, in particular?

Nicole: … Yes. … I think what I've really taken away is the idea that I've given myself that I've got nothing to look forward to, and looking at that and questioning is that true or not. I really think digging down into that bit I've really taken away.

Windy: And this dynamic of feeling a child and being an adult, you brought echoes of that in what we were talking about as well.

Nicole: Yeah.

Windy: So that's going to be something that we'll look at in the future. How would you like to go forward? As I say, we could either make another appointment now, we can call it quits now, if you like, and say, 'That's it, I'm done,' or you can put it into practice, see how it goes and then contact me at a time that suits you best. How would you like to go forward?

[In SST, the offer excludes the client making an appointment at the end of the session because SST includes the period where the client reflects on their learning from the session, digests this learning, takes suitable action and sees what happened before deciding whether or not to make an appointment. In BTISSTM, the offer is up to six sessions over a six-month period and the client is in full control concerning how many sessions to have and when to have them. Therefore, in BTISSTM, the offer includes making an appointment at the end of the session.]

Nicole: I think I'm quite happy to make an appointment now for next week. I'll be … just over a week into my experiment, but then also preparing myself for going back to work.

Windy: OK. That's perfectly fine. Is there anything else you want to say that you wished you might have told me on this issue that you haven't said or anything you want to ask that you may wish you had asked me before we close?

[These are typical questions to ask in SST at the end of a session.]

Nicole: No, I don't think so.

Windy: So I'm going to stop the recording, which I'll send to you and then I'll get it transcribed, send that to you when it's transcribed. Then you can think of a name that you'd like to go by.

Nicole: Yeah.

Windy: No rush on that issue.

Nicole: No worries.

Preamble

As discussed in Chapter 3, before the second and subsequent sessions of BTISSTM, the client is sent a pre-session form (see Appendix 3). This is designed to help them review the progress they have made since they had their previous session and prepare from the upcoming session so that they can get the most from it. I encourage them to return the form to me so that I can help them to best effect during the session. Nicole's pre-session form that she submitted before the second session is found in Appendix 8.

5

Session 2

Date: *04/08/23*
Time: *46 minutes 44 secs*

Windy: Hi Nicole, how are you today?

Nicole: Yeah, I'm OK, thank you.

Windy: Good. So, we're gonna focus on the second issue that you were talking about. Before we do that let's find out a little bit more about what you did as a result of what we discussed last time.

[In BTISSTM, the client can bring up a number of issues over the course of therapy and it is important for the therapist to keep track of how much progress they are making on each issue and what they did to promote such change. Hence, my question to Nicole.]

Nicole: Yep. So, yeah, we went away for the week. So one of the things that I took away from our last session was … a challenge to myself that I'm gonna have one pudding and I'm not gonna go back for more, which is what I know I would do and it is what I wanted to do. But I didn't. I did just have the one.

Windy: How did you manage that?

Nicole:	... [*Long pause*] I kind of said to myself, 'Well, you can have another one tomorrow. So you don't need another one right now.'
Windy:	So you could delay your gratification, in other words.
Nicole:	Yeah.... [*Pause*] I think it's because I saw it as like a challenge ... [*pause*] and I kind of ... [*pause*], I don't know, I'd already pre-empted that that's what I was gonna do, and I did it.
Windy:	Sorry, you 'pre-empted'? How do you mean?
Nicole:	As in like before we went away and after our session I was like, 'Right, well, that's my challenge. That's what I'm gonna do.'
Windy:	So you saw it as a challenge and you made a decision that you were gonna react in a certain way.
Nicole:	Yeah.
Windy:	OK. And those are the important ingredients: 'This is a challenge for me and this is how I'm gonna respond to the challenge.'
	[*This is my summary of the important ingredients that led to Nicole's progress on this issue.*]
Nicole:	Yeah.
Windy:	OK. One of the things that I think is important in therapy is to capitalise on things like that. So maybe we can actually utilise those ingredients, so to speak, and utilise them in other areas that we talk

about. I think you were gonna mention a 'but' there somewhere. Was there a but?

Nicole: Yeah, kind of. So I saw that as that's my challenge; that's what I'm going to do. I made a decision to do that. But I guess what I hadn't thought about is what about the rest of the time around that. What about in the evening when we're sat in the new apartment? Because I then ate chocolate then. So it was like I did the one thing that I said I was going to do but I didn't really ... take that further, if that makes sense.

Windy: I see. So it was a localised thing.

Nicole: Yes.

Windy: 'This is my challenge with respect to the one dessert or two desserts. So this is my challenge, this is what I'm going to be doing.' So, I guess the question is to what extent can you generalise that to other areas with respect to eating? To what extent could you see choosing to have whatever chocolate you would feel would be healthy for you to have, seeing that as a challenge, making a decision about dealing with that so that it's not just localised?

[Here, I am suggesting that Nicole could generalise her learning to other relevant episodes.]

Nicole: Yeah. It's like my brain worked around, it's like, 'Well, that's fine.'

Windy: It's funny you say that. Many years ago I worked in a private psychiatric hospital and the secretary was talking and she was saying that she was struggling with dealing with chocolate. And I said, 'Do you have any chocolate?' She said, 'Yeah.' I said, 'Can I have a piece?' and she gave me a piece and I kind of marked it and I put it on the top of her computer screen. I said, 'Right, every week I'm gonna come back, I want to see that chocolate there.' And every week I came back and that chocolate was there. However, it didn't generalise to other chocolates that she had.

Nicole: Yeah.

Windy: Do you see what we're talking about?

Nicole: Yeah.

Windy: So I'm wondering what you could actually do about that. Is that something that you could say, 'OK, I've got the ingredients, I have an opportunity to generalise that. Do I want to take advantage of that?'

Nicole: Yeah, I do, and I feel like perhaps doing it one thing at a time might be the way for me to go, because I don't think I've ever tried that before. Like on holiday the one thing was the one pudding, and I did that, saved myself some calories with that. And then the next challenge could be adding to that.

[Nicole is suggesting that generalisation can take place one step at a time.]

Windy: Right. The chocolate, you mean?

Nicole: Yeah.

Windy: That's right. And that fits in. Single-session therapy, which informs the work we're doing, is sometimes called One-At-A-Time, and one thing it mentions is one session at a time. One foodstuff at a time might be something for you to think about.

Nicole: Yeah.

Windy: So maybe you can start thinking about and maybe writing down the order in which you want to tackle these things.

Nicole: Yeah, that sounds good.

Windy: I'll leave you to do that.

Nicole: Yeah.

Windy: Shall we get onto the second issue?

[It would have been better for me to ask Nicole if she wanted to add anything to the discussion rather than getting onto the second issue.]

Nicole: Yeah.

Windy: Which is what you originally gave the heading Imposter Syndrome and what you said here about you want to feel good enough by the end of the session and learn how to deal with being busy without getting overwhelmed and to be OK with not knowing everything and not being perfect. Are those linked, those two, or are they separate: dealing with being overwhelmed and not knowing everything? Are they linked in some way?

[Here, I am reading from Nicole's preparation form for the second session. Remember that clients are

asked to prepare for every session that they have in BTISSTM.]

Nicole: … Yeah, I think it's all linked because, when I feel not good enough, then I … wanna read more or listen to more, do more things to … learn more, so then I feel good enough, but I never feel good enough and I always feel like an imposter.

Windy: And that's your go-to attempt to solve the problem: do more, read more?

Nicole: Yes, or I can go the other way and do nothing, and then it's the same outcome: I don't feel good enough because I've done nothing or I've read this but I still don't feel good enough.

Windy: Yeah. So it sounds like doing nothing doesn't help you because it doesn't lead you to change anything.

Nicole: Yeah.

Windy: And doing more leads to the overwhelm. Do you think you get to the heart of the problem doing more? Because it's based on the idea, 'If I know more, I can solve the problem by this.'

[In my mind, I am thinking that Nicole's attempts to solve the problem only serve to maintain it. I raise this in my next but one response below that begins, 'Right, yeah'.]

Nicole: Well … knowledge is power, I feel like. Knowledge is confidence.

Windy: Sure.

Nicole: If I know within myself I know what I'm doing, I'm confident I've mastered that skill or whatever it is, then... that solves it.

Windy: Right, yeah. It's a tricky situation in a way because you're right, if you know more, knowing more is a good thing. The question is does knowing more solve the imposter syndrome problem or does it, somehow in a subtle way, reinforce it?

Nicole: ... [*Pause*] I think it reinforces it because, even when I read more, learn more, I feel like ... I haven't got a really good memory and I'm not one of these people who soaks up information like a sponge and then they know it. I have to do something several times to then know it. I feel like I'm quite a slow learner.... I don't feel like I ever really get it.

Windy: Right. So you've got this state which I guess we could call being able to get it and you don't reach that stage.

Nicole: Yeah.

Windy: So help me to understand what is that stage of getting it? What is it for you?

Nicole: ... [*Long pause*] I think I was specifically talking about my work and ... [*long pause*] with clients not feeling like I get it or not feeling like I know enough stuff. I don't know if I'm answering the question right. Can you ask it again so that I'm with you?

Windy: You spoke about a state which you don't have.

Nicole: Yeah.

Windy: You say, 'I don't get it.' So, if you don't get something, there is a state that's somehow in your mind that would be equivalent to getting it. Maybe we can use a specific example to really see if we can clarify a little bit. Now, can you think about a specific example where maybe you're with a client or at work where you don't get it and you have this idea about what getting it would look like and feel like?

[In BTISSTM, as in SST, a specific example often serves to elucidate the issue that is being discussed.]

Nicole: Yeah. So, I can think of an example this week with a client.

Windy: OK. So, tell me a little bit about that.

Nicole: … *[Pause]* So it was a new client, and she said what she wanted from me and the sessions, and I felt like it wasn't something that I can provide, but then I don't know if I can provide that or not because I've never really worked in that way.

Windy: So, can I ask you what she wanted from you?

Nicole: She wanted me to … *[pause]* – I'm just trying to think of what it was exactly she said … *[pause]* like somebody to challenge her and not somebody who really just listens and reflects the whole time, but somebody who challenges. And I don't feel like I'm that kind of … *[pause]* counsellor.

Windy: OK, because you were trained not to challenge?

Nicole: No. So I was trained integratively. I have challenged and I do challenge.... So I don't know why I was like, 'Well, I can't do that.' I didn't say that.

Windy: But that's what you thought.

Nicole: Yeah ... because I'm more comfortable listening.

Windy: Right, OK.

Nicole: So that's easy.

Windy: So you're more comfortable listening. She wanted the challenge. You have challenged before, but your initial reaction was, 'I can't do that.'

Nicole: Yeah.

Windy: OK. And did you stay in that initial reaction or did you shift from it?

Nicole: I think I ... [*pause*] probably stayed in it ... and have stayed in it and thought, 'Well, I don't know I if I can ... do this.'

Windy: Now, when you've challenged before, did you have the same process: that you thought you couldn't challenge and then you challenged and then you recognised that you could challenge?

Nicole: Sometimes I can easily do it and other times ... [*pause*] I sit with it for about five, ten minutes, or however long, I don't know, and I think, 'Right, shall I bring this up? Shall I challenge about this?' and then I do. I don't think there's really been a time where I haven't because I then externalise it and think, 'Well, it's actually best for the client if I do. Stop worrying about you. This is not about you,' sort of thing.

Windy: Right. So, again, it's interesting, isn't it, that we're also talking about the theme of generalising from one situation to another situation. So it sounds like that there are times when you can challenge and you can challenge fairly quickly and naturally.

Nicole: Yep.

Windy: There are other times that you kind of struggle but then you sit with it and then you do challenge. With this client, though, your process was, 'She wants me to challenge her. I'm not comfortable doing that.'

[At this point in the session, I am striving to understand the important factors in the example.]

Nicole: I also feel, not just with her but with other people, like a power imbalance, like I'm somehow lower than other people; that I'm … [*pause*] not up to their standards.

[Nicole's response adds a new factor.]

Windy: What standard did this client have that you weren't up to?

Nicole: … [*Long pause*] I just felt like I needed to be more.

Windy: To be more?

Nicole: Yeah.

Windy: To be more what?

Nicole: … [*Pause*] Of a professional. I'm a counsellor. I'm a qualified counsellor, but I don't feel like I am, and how has that even happened?

Windy: If you felt like a qualified counsellor in that situation, what would be different?

Nicole: I wouldn't be sat there worrying about … 'Well, can I challenge her?' I would just do. I would just be.

Windy: So it would be effortless, like it has been in the past.

Nicole: Yeah.

Windy: And you weren't.

Nicole: Yeah.

Windy: You naturally felt, 'Look, I can't do this,' and then you started to think, 'Wait, I'm not a professional counsellor, because professional counsellors would have no doubts about that. They would go straight into it.'

Nicole: Yeah, exactly.

Windy: How long have you been a counsellor for?

Nicole: So, I've been qualified for six months. I'm new.

Windy: I know you didn't, but what do you think would've happened if you had thought like this: 'OK, my natural reaction is to not challenge. I can challenge because I've challenged in the past. Sometimes I've done it effortlessly, sometimes I haven't. But I'm not natural, but this is something where I'm new? If you'd have thought like that in the situation, what impact, if any, would that have made to you?

Nicole: Not much, I think, because I feel like this person and other people need more than what I can provide.

Windy: Right, but you can provide her with challenges because you have provided other people with challenges.

Nicole: Yeah.

Windy: But it sounds to me that somehow the standard that you have is, 'A professional counsellor effortlessly would challenge, would have no doubt.'

Nicole: Yeah, and would have confidence in their abilities in themselves.

Windy: Yeah, exactly. 'And I didn't feel like that and therefore,' what? What's the conclusion for you?

Nicole: I'm not good enough.

Windy: Right, OK. Good enough as what?

Nicole: A counsellor.

Windy: Yeah, OK. Can I give you my take on this?

[I am aware that we are approaching the halfway point in the session, and my attempts to tease solutions from Nicole are not bearing as much fruit as I would like. Thus, I decide to ask Nicole if she would like to hear my 'take' on this issue.]

Nicole: Yeah.

[*My take is based on some ideas from Rational Emotive Behaviour Therapy that informs a lot, but not all, of my therapeutic work.*]

Windy: So it sounds to me that you've got a state in mind which we can call the professional counselling state where you're confident, and that's how you'd like to be. Is that right?

Nicole: Yeah.

Windy: And, if this had any power [*showing her a magic wand that I have to hand for occasions such as this*], I would wave it and say, 'This is going to be instant confidence for Nicole,' and I would. I don't like to see you suffer, but this ain't a magic wand. We're putting it away and we're gonna have to deal with it more psychologically. So, 'I'd like to be confident right from the start like any professional counsellor,' and that's what you'd like.

Nicole: Yeah, but when you say that it sounds quite unreasonable to think that of myself.

Windy: Wait a minute, I haven't finished yet.

Nicole: Sorry. I've come to my own conclusion with it.

Windy: So that's what we call your desire and that's fine. I mean, there's nothing wrong with wanting instant confidence. That's fine. The question is the attitude then that you bring to the table, there are only two possibilities and I'll go over them both for you. And they both start off exactly the same way: 'I'd like to have the confidence of a professional counsellor. I am a professional counsellor and I'd like to be confident, no doubt. That's what I'd like. That's the state I want.' Attitude 1: 'And therefore I have to be like that and, if I'm not, I'm not good enough.' Attitude 2: 'Yes, I'd like to feel like that, but I don't always have to feel like that and, if I'm not, that's a pity, but it doesn't mean that I'm not good enough. It means that I haven't got the confidence that I want, and let's see if I can dispassionately find out how I can practise so that I can get the confidence.' Now, which attitude do you think you were operating on?

[*Here I am outlining the difference between Nicole holding a rigid attitude ('Attitude 1') and a flexible attitude ('Attitude 2').*]

Nicole: The first one.

Windy: Yeah. Now, what would it be like if you really believed the second, Nicole?

Nicole: It feels like a pressure is taken off.

Windy: Yeah, OK.

Nicole: I'm thinking of the overwhelm there as well – because the pressure's there, I get overwhelmed.

Windy: The overwhelm comes as a result of you thinking that, 'I need to know more.' But in this case, this is an attitude problem, and an attitude problem is not gonna be solved by knowledge. Increased knowledge is a good thing. I'm not arguing that you stop finding out about new things by any manner or means, but this is not going to solve the attitude problem, because it's an attitude problem. Basically, it is a question of are you gonna be rigid about your desires or are you going to be flexible about them?

Nicole: Flexible as in?

Windy: 'I'd like to be confident but it's not necessary. I don't have to. There's no law which says I have to be like that.

Nicole: Yeah.

Windy: Once you get into a flexible frame of mind, then you can get access to a question like I'm going to ask you now: out of 100 counsellors who have been trained for six months how many of them have instant confidence in all areas?

Nicole: Probably 1%.

Windy: That's right. The reason I don't ask that question when you're in a rigid frame of mind, because your answer will be influenced by rigidity.

Nicole: And I'd probably say all of them.

Windy: Yeah, exactly, because you then create the idea, and that's how you end up, I think probably in this area and other areas of your life, what you said; that you feel childlike, because, 'The adult state, I've gotta have that.'

Nicole: Yeah.

Windy: Does that sound like something that you might find useful to take forward, working on becoming more flexible about your desires?

[*Having outlined my REBT-informed 'take' on Nicole's issue, I ask her if she might find this helpful to take forward.*]

Nicole: It is, yeah.

Windy: So the way you do that is by, I think preparing yourself, actually. Do you prepare yourself before a session?

Nicole: Yeah, I do.

Windy: How do you prepare yourself before a counselling session? Let me find out.

Nicole: So, if it's a new client, I clear my mind. I'll sit here for ten minutes at the computer before the session and I do deep breathing exercises because that brings me into the moment, because otherwise I'll get worked up and then I'll be really nervous and then it won't work, bringing a nervous counsellor on. And I can do that quite well. I feel like I've mastered that.

Windy: Because you've been practising it?

Nicole: Yeah.

Windy: What were you like when you first started to practise that?

Nicole: … Yeah, it took a while to master it, so I wasn't perfect to begin with.

Windy: So you had the experience of actually doing something that was going to be helpful to you that you started off with that you're not proficient about, but then you practised it and, after practice you became more proficient and then you had the benefits of it.

Nicole: Yeah.

Windy: I don't want to interfere with that because it sounds like that's an important thing for you to do. What I'm wondering about is can you prepare to go into counselling sessions in the way that we've been talking about: 'Obviously, I want to be confident but I don't have to be. If I'm not, then that's a pity, but it doesn't mean that I'm less than the client or less than any other therapist. It just means that I need to think a little bit more about what it is I'm not confident about, see if I can find out, like I have in the past. Yeah, I've been able to use that.' Now, as I say, I don't want to interfere with a successful intervention, but is that something that you might be able to bring into your preparation?

Nicole: Yeah, although I feel like it's more after the fact that I need that mindset. So beforehand I feel like I've got my thing, I know how to make myself get into a state that I need to do counselling. It's more after where I don't do it but it's more like I slam my head on the desk and I'm like, 'Ugh! What was that? Why did I say that?' or, 'Why did I do that?'

Windy: So are you saying then that you feel less than or not good enough after the fact? You're not experiencing that during the session?

Nicole: … [*Pause*] Yeah, I do experience it during as well. So during and after, but not every time and not with every client.

Windy: No. My view about this is this: either before or after you have an opportunity to do some preparation along the lines that I'm talking about, like, 'I don't have to be confident all the time. I'm new.' But in the moment you might need just a phrase that comes into your mind that reminds you of that and will deal with the same issue, a phrase or a word or something like that.

Nicole: Before we started the session I've got some empowerment cards that I used to rotate every now and again, depending on what I needed. And I haven't opened them since I moved here, so five months. And I opened them before the session and I picked one, and it's quite fitting, I think.

Windy: Do you want to show it to me?

Nicole: It says: 'You already have what it takes.'

Windy: Right. And, in this context, that means what to you, as you as a counsellor?

Nicole: It means, even before I was a counsellor, I had what it took... [*pause*] and it's just been built on. And I know I am good at it and I do have what it takes.

Windy: Yeah, that's right, but I would add: 'But there are going to be times when I don't know what to do.'

[*Nicole's card does not help her to deal with the adversity of not knowing what to do. I bring that to her attention.*]

Nicole: Yeah.

Windy: And you can incorporate that as well: 'And then I can learn about that. But the 'not knowing what to do' just means I don't know what to do. It doesn't mean I'm not good enough.' So, I don't know how that would get distilled into a pithy statement, but I think that's your task.

Nicole: Yeah.

Windy: In the moment.

Nicole: Yeah. I think that's something that I can figure out; what is it that I can say to myself ... that would, I guess, remind me or bring me back to, 'It's fine. I don't have to know everything and feel confident right now.'

                 [*Nicole is showing that she gets the point I have been making which is helping her to develop a healthy attitude towards not knowing everything and not feeling confident.*]

Windy: That's right. 'I don't have to have instant confidence and instant knowledge right now.' Then afterwards you could then say, 'Well, how many new counsellors do?' Do you have a support group at all of counsellors and new counsellors?

Nicole: ... Yeah. So I've got a friend who I chat to. We're both at the same stage; we're both setting up private practice and things like that, so we kind of support each other. I have group supervision as well which is useful. But I guess I don't have a group of new counsellors that I ... chat to.

Windy: I think that's a shame because I think that that might also be an opportunity to see the struggles that other people have, because I think, when you're in that frame of mind, 'I should know how to deal with this,' as you say, 'The rest of the other people can do it,' so you construct out of your attitude the scenario that, 'Other new counsellors are much more confident than me.' Now, some are. You're in a private practice, are you?

[Here, I am drawing on the SST principle of helping the client to call upon helpful external resources.]

Nicole: Yeah, I'm setting up, just starting.

Windy: I think probably four or five times I've dealt with people who've been reluctant to set up a private practice because of this issue. Now, you've set one up, so that says something, doesn't it?

Nicole: Yeah.

Windy: What does it say?

Nicole: ... *[Pause]* That I'm ready, that I know, at some level, that ... *[long pause]* I can provide a service and take payment for a service that is good enough for that.

Windy: That's right. Again, if you can build upon that, because these other people are really saying, 'I have to be confident before I set up the private practice,' and that's a good trick.

Nicole: Yeah, how are they going to do it?

Windy: 'I'm going to have to be confident swimming before
             I get into the water.' So I think that, if you can
             capitalise on that, 'I've actually come forward.
             I'm prepared to enter into something and be able to put
             up with scenarios which I may not be able to deal
             with. Now I've got the opportunity to say, "Look, I
             don't need to have this instant knowledge and
             instant confidence."' That's what imposter
             syndrome is: 'I have to have the confidence and the
             knowledge that I fantasise other people in my
             situation.'

             [*Here, I make the point that Nicole is already taking
             important behavioural steps, which the issue with
             which she is struggling has not stopped her from
             making. She can then add to these behavioural steps
             the flexible attitude that we have been discussing.*]

Nicole: Yeah.

Windy: Basically, they're saying, 'I have to have the
             knowledge and the confidence of people who've
             been in the field for years.'

Nicole: That would be good. If there's something that I
             could buy and have, then I'd do it.

Windy: Indeed. Unfortunately, there's a long waiting list for
             it. It's a bit like an assessment for ADHD – I've
             waited a long time for that one.

Nicole: Yeah.

Windy: Does that feel like something like we're getting to
             the heart of the problem of what you've previously
             called the imposter syndrome?

Nicole: ... [*Pause*] Yes.

Windy: There's a hesitation there.

Nicole: So I feel like, yes ... I'm just thinking ... so it's a confidence thing ... and that's OK to not be confident, and, when I think about times before when I've not been ready because I'm not confident to do something, and I've had to do it for college or whatever, then I've done it, it ... adds to growth.

Windy: That's right.

Nicole: It's scary.

Windy: Yeah, and you did it without the benefit of the flexible attitude. So, even though you had the same attitude, and I think that's what's coming across to me already with you, is you're not going to let the issue stop you from doing things that are important to you.

Nicole: Yeah.

Windy: Would you say that's a strength of yours?

                [*In BTISSTM, as in SST, I look for the client's strengths and bring these to the table as I do here.*]

Nicole: Yeah. Just do it scared.

Windy: That's right. What I'm saying is you can do it with healthy concern rather than scared, because the scared comes from the idea, 'Oh my God, I hope I don't get a client that I don't know how to deal with, because I have to be confident,' as opposed to, 'Well, obviously I don't want to do that but, if I do, then that's unfortunate. I don't have to be confident. I don't have to be knowledgeable. I can learn from this.'

Nicole: Yeah. I feel like I've gone from terrified – I'd say it's more than scared, like terrified at the beginning to what you said: like a healthy concern. It has progressed as I've gone on.

Windy: Right. Now, the other thing is, because we've got six sessions, and since you like a challenge, just think about how you can generalise this to other areas where this crops up for you.

[*As we are moving to the final part of the session, I want to see if Nicole can generalise this learning to other areas of her life.*]

Nicole: Yeah. It crops up everywhere.

Windy: Any particular other areas that come to mind that don't involve counselling, for example?

Nicole: So with other people, like my partner's parents... [pause] or his family, I don't feel good enough.

Windy: Right, OK.

Nicole: In my other job that I do – I'm a receptionist ... [*pause*] actually, no, I feel good enough there. Let's take that away. But in previous jobs, I feel like I don't ever feel good enough.

Windy: Well, let's have a look. I think we've got time to see if we can generalise what we've discussed here. Can you choose another area that might be useful for us to briefly look at to see how you can generalise that?

Nicole: … [*Pause*] I'd say my partner's friends and family.

Windy: OK. Give me a scenario that captures that issue specifically.

Nicole: So … something that's already happened?

Windy: Or something that might be cropping up.

Nicole: So something, I guess, that happened before was … I met my partner's friend and his wife and we went for lunch, and I saw myself as 'guess the imposter', as the outsider, the runt of the litter is a good way of describing it.

Windy: OK. Now, what would have had to have been in place for you not to feel that?

Nicole: … [*Long pause*] Confidence in myself. I don't know.… If I describe them and then I describe me, I wonder if I can get there.

Windy: OK.

Nicole: So my partner, he's a professional, he's got a good job, earns good money. The same with his friend and his friend's wife. I feel like they all grew up in a very traditional, standard way, never really had any big sort of life problems – mum, dad, 2.4 children, college, university and then got a good job, like normal people, and I don't feel like I'm that at all.

Windy: Because you grew up with what?

Nicole: … Trouble and adversity and … [*pause*] stuff that happened.

Windy: So what they're bringing to the lunch is what or to the event?

Nicole: I feel like we're just different…, I want to say breeds of people. It's funny because I say 'runt of the litter' and 'breeds of people'. I feel like they're bringing… [long pause] I don't know.

Windy: If you were to draw them and draw you in terms of worth, what would that picture look like? Have you got any paper there?

[I am not sure what prompted me to suggest this, but sometimes having a client draw how they see themselves in relation to others can be useful.]

Nicole: I have, yeah.

Windy: Why don't you quickly do that?

Nicole: … [*Pause*] Draw them.

Windy: In terms of worth, in terms of size, and then draw you.

Nicole: … [*Long pause*] I can't draw very well.

Windy: That's alright. I'm not going to ask you to draw a line.

Nicole: … [*Long pause*] I don't know if you're gonna be able to see it.

Windy: Right. So there's you on the right-hand side and smaller?

Nicole: Yeah.

Windy: And there's a distance between you and them.

Nicole: Yeah.

Windy: Now, what I'd like you to do is I'd like you to draw you the same size and the same distance between people so that you're part of a four rather than a three and one.

[Once a client has drawn how they see their problem, it is useful to have them draw the solution; in this case being an equal part of the group of four people.]

Nicole: … *[Long pause]* I'm there.

Windy: Now, what would you have to think in order to reflect the second one?

Nicole: … *[Pause]* I think it's brought something up.

[Making the second drawing has brought up an important issue for Nicole – see Figure 1 below.]

Windy: OK, what's it brought up for you?

Nicole: … *[Long pause]* I think I see the little me as… me as a child and, when I put me beside them, I kind of felt like I was abandoning her. So it's a lot, isn't it? Sorry.

Windy: No, that's fine. So I think the question is that I'd like you think about as we approach the end of our session is: 'How can I preserve my equality with other people while still having a connection to that child and not abandoning her?' Do you think you'd be able to think about that?

[*Here, I encourage Nicole to think about how she can feel equal to others without abandoning the child in her.*]

Nicole: Yeah, I'd be able to think about it.

Windy: The other thing I'd like to suggest is that maybe you could take a picture of those pictures and maybe we could include them in the book, if you're willing.

Nicole: Yeah.

Figure 1 Nicole's drawing

Windy: So I think what would be useful if we could have them separate: the one with the three and the small one, and the second one. Then I think people will understand more clearly. But I think that's an important thing. It's almost like, 'I don't want to abandon this child part of me. So I can't really see myself as equal. So that's the task: how can I see myself as equal without abandoning that?' So that's what I'm gonna suggest.

Nicole: Yeah. It's a good thing to think about.

Windy: So continue with the work done on I think what you call the overeating, continue what we talked about in terms of the imposter syndrome. When I send you the next form, what I'm gonna be doing is I'm gonna list the issue here for you so it's clear. So I'll make a modification of that. So is there anything that I said to you today that was off-putting or you wish you hadn't said?

Nicole: No. I feel like it's good work done. I feel like I'll be taking away some stuff and some stuff to think about and to ponder on between sessions as well.

Windy: So, again, as before, I'm gonna give you complete carte blanche in terms of when you have the third session. I don't know whether you want to nominate that now or you want to put this into practice and think about it. I'll be completely guided by you.

Nicole: I'm quite busy next week and I don't know what I'm doing the week after either. So I'll probably email you and just... get something in a couple of weeks when I know what I'm doing.

Windy: OK, great.

Nicole: Alright, thank you.

Windy: Thank you, bye.

Preamble

As discussed in Chapter 3 and the Preamble to Chapter 5, before the second and subsequent sessions of BTISSTM, the client is sent a pre-session form (see Appendix 3). This is designed to help them review the progress they have made since they had their previous session and prepare from the upcoming session so that they can get the most from it. I encourage them to return the form to me so that I can help them to best effect during the session. Nicole's pre-session form that she submitted before the third session is found in Appendix 9.

6

Session 3

Date: *22/08/23*
Time: *40 minutes 20 secs*

Windy: OK, so Session 3.

Nicole: Yep.

Windy: It sounds like you made a good deal of progress on the imposter syndrome.

Nicole: Yeah.

Windy: My reading of it was that I think you were integrating the adult and the kid part of yourself, rather than anything else. Does that make sense?

Nicole: Yeah. And I guess I wasn't aware of that until I did that drawing of ... why I was feeling like that – was actually because, I guess ... the younger me was showing up rather than adult me.

Windy: Right.

Nicole: That's what it feels like.

Windy: Yeah.

Nicole: And I wasn't aware I was doing this but, after our last session for the whole weekend I watched kids' films; I watched Harry Potter all weekend. I'd never seen it before but I really fancied it.

Windy: And what's your take on that?

Nicole: … It kind of felt like I just needed to escape from the adult world into a magical kid's world of some description. I think it was only after the third day when I was watching it I was like … 'I think I know what's going on. I feel like I need a bit of escapism and this has really helped.' Then I wondered if I did that more often if that might help… adult me be more present as an adult if I give time and space to younger me.

Windy: Well, that's a good hypothesis. We'll see how that works out down the line.

Nicole: Yeah.

Windy: Is there anything else you want to say about that particular issue?

Nicole: … Not at the moment. I think it's still marinating.

Windy: So we'll let it marinate and we'll have a look at what you first called overeating and weight gain. Now, we focused on that on our first session and I think, in preparation for the second session, you wondered if looking at the other issue would have an impact on the overeating. What do you make of that connection now?

Nicole: … Well, nothing's changed with the eating, so I'm sure if … [*pause*] that's helped in any way. I feel like this overeating thing … I feel like it's never gonna change, like it's gonna be a forever thing. I don't know how to shift that. And I'm quite emotional today.

Windy: About the issue or what?

Nicole: No.... [*Pause*] I don't think it's about that. It's just I'm overly emotional today, so I knew I was going to cry at some point. No, I've got tinnitus and I suffer with migraines.... [*Pause*] And I've really been suffering with it.

Windy: Right.

Nicole: Just feeling hypersensitive.

Windy: Sure. Do you want to deal with the focus of the overeating today or what?

Nicole: ... Yeah, because I wonder if overeating and how I treat my body by what I put in it affects all these different things, like the tinnitus that I've got. There's no known cause for it. I've been to the doctor's, I've ... had hearing tests and stuff and there's no solution or anything to it. And the migraines as well ... there's no reason for it, and I wonder if I treated my body better and was healthier, if that would help. I wonder if it's my body screaming at me. That's what the tinnitus feels like. It's a high-pitched tone.

Windy: Your tinnitus is indicating what to you through its high-pitched noise?

Nicole: It's like, 'Stop ... treating me like this. Stop ... [*pause*] putting crap in your body.'

[Nicole is speculating about the connection between what she calls 'overeating' and her tinnitus and migraine.]

Windy: So, on the one hand, you want to change that; you're interpreting some of the symptoms that you're getting as indications that you need to start treating your body well. On the other hand, there's a sense of hopelessness that you're always going to be this way.

Nicole: Yeah. And it doesn't make sense.... A couple of years ago I went for an all-round check of everything in my body, like one of those that you pay for and they tell you how healthy you are. And I was hoping, which sounds really odd and I feel really bad for this, but I was hoping that they'd say, 'You've got prediabetes,' or, 'You've got high blood pressure,' or, 'You've got something and it's down to eating.' And then that would make me shift. I feel like it needs to be something big like that to then make me.

Windy: It's almost like a health warning.

[Nicole is speculating that she needs some kind of health warning to make her change her eating habits.]

Nicole: Yeah.

Windy: 'You need to take care of yourself.' If there was that, what do you think you would do?

Nicole: I'd be really pissed off with myself that I didn't do something before it got to the point where there was stuff going on.

Windy: Right, and what would you do going forward?

Nicole: I would change.

Windy: You would change what?

Nicole: Probably instantly ... what I eat.

Windy: What would you change?

Nicole: I would change what I eat, I would exercise.

Windy: Right.

Nicole: I know it would be an instant thing.

Windy: So it sounds like on the one hand you feel hopeless about changing that, on the other hand it sounds like you would not think too much about it; you would instantly change, as you say, and bring about a change that you feel hopeless about if that warning wasn't there.

Nicole: Yeah.

Windy: So what do you conclude from that?

Nicole: ... [*Long pause*] I guess that's maybe why I'm trying to make a connection between the tinnitus and the migraines, to be like, 'This is your body telling you that you need to do something different; that it's not happy and healthy,' and maybe that'll kick me into something. I think it kind of came to a head today, this morning, because I woke up and my eyelids were puffy because of the migraines, my tinnitus is bad, and I just laid in the bath and cried for about half an hour. And I haven't really got to that point yet with the tinnitus and migraines apart from today. I've reached my limit.

Windy: Right. Are you saying that things need to be bad enough for you to change?

Nicole: Yeah.

Windy: And are you saying that you're approaching that?

Nicole: Yeah, I think so.

Windy: When you stand back and you think about that as a reason to change, what do you think?

Nicole: … [*Pause*] I think it's … [*pause*] sad that I have to get to a point … to do that.

Windy: Yeah, right. Would you like a different way forward?

Nicole: I would but I don't know what that is and I feel like I've been searching for it forever.

Windy: Well, that's why we're here, isn't it?

Nicole: Yeah.

Windy: Searching forever for what, Nicole?

Nicole: … For a shift in mindset or a shift in something.

Windy: And what kinds of shifts have you tried and what have been the outcome of those shifts?

Nicole: I've tried ... dieting, calorie-counting.

Windy: Let's have a look at what you've tried but let's link it to the mindset that you're identifying as being really quite important.

Nicole: I don't know where the mindset comes from before.

Windy: What's the dieting mindset? When you're on a diet, what's the mindset that goes along with that?

Nicole: ... [*Long pause*] It was more to do with looks and how I looked, and I'd get to a point where I'd reach a certain weight, think, 'Right, that's it.' I'd look in the mirror and feel disgusting and then it's like my mindset changes to, 'Right, we need to sort this out and look better.'

Windy: So two things there that strike me: one is the attractiveness mindset you're being motivated by, but also the idea of what you've come to, like, 'OK, that's it, I've reached my limit here,' like you taking action.

Nicole: Yeah.

Windy: 'OK, that's it. I've reached my limit,' almost. How has the attractiveness mindset been working for you?

Nicole: I feel like that's gone because my ... partner loves me unconditionally and ... I'm not so concerned with how I look anymore.

Windy: Right. So are you saying that if you didn't have a partner that would be different?

Nicole: If I didn't have a partner and I was then going to want to be dating, then, yeah, that would probably be different.

Windy: Right. So it's almost like 'Well, my partner loves me, so it doesn't really matter what I look like' kind of thing.

Nicole: Yeah.

Windy: 'I'm not going out there. I'm not trying to–'

Nicole: Impress anyone.

Windy: So what other mindsets or what other things have you tried and what mindsets have gone along with?

               [As is typical in BTISSTM and SST, I am reviewing what Nicole has tried before to deal with her 'overeating' issue.]

Nicole: So, when we had Covid, I had Covid right at the beginning and I really suffered with it, and they said that people that are overweight will suffer more, and that terrified me because I've had health anxiety in the past and it's probably something I still struggle with. And that was like a mindset shift. I was like, 'Right, I need to get healthy.' And I got really healthy, actually. I was able to run for half an hour straight. I did the Couch to 5K. I lost a lot of weight. I was eating healthy. And then it just changed when Covid went.

Windy: So it's like fear-based?

Nicole: Yeah.

Windy: It's like what I call the healthy mindset but like a fear.

Nicole: Yeah, very much based on the fear.

Windy: So motivated by fear. And you were able to initiate a change both of diet and exercise.

Nicole: Yeah.

Windy: And you lost a lot of weight, and then what?

Nicole: And then, as I said, Covid fizzled out, went away and I feel like with that so did that mindset. And, since that mindset shifted again, I haven't been able to find something. Again, I get into that.

[*Nicole has indicated a number of times that she has brought about healthy changes in her diet by holding a fear-based mindset.*]

Windy: You said here how you've tried to deal with the issue we're talking about. You said, 'All sorts: CBT, group work, diet.' So let's have a look at the CBT. What was that? Was that CBT for weight loss?

Nicole: Yeah and it was … when the thought comes up of, 'I want to go and have a chocolate bar or something, what can you do differently?' Riding the wave of the … [*pause*] intenseness of wanting to go and grab for it. It was giving me tools and techniques of what I can do in the moment.

Windy: What kind of tools and techniques did you have?

Nicole: So, riding the wave. I remember having a sheet of a hundred different things that I could do instead of eating, but – I think I said this to you before, none of them really did the same as what a chocolate bar would do.

Windy: It didn't have that ingredient that the chocolate bar gave you.

Nicole: Yeah.

Windy: What kinds of things were on the list? Can you give me an example?

Nicole: Lighting a candle, having a bath, listening to music.

Windy: We could say those techniques don't hold a candle to the chocolate bar.

Nicole: Yeah.

Windy: But it's basically saying, it seems to me, 'Get your comfort differently. Rely on some other sense.'

Nicole: Yeah.

Windy: Were you able to do that?

Nicole: Not particularly, no.

Windy: You weren't lighting a candle while eating the chocolate bar?

Nicole: No. The CBT didn't really feel…

Windy: In a sense, it's about approaching a particular difficulty that you have or most people have, dealing with urges to have something that you really like which is not good for you. It's not embedded in a mindset. You haven't said you did it for health or for looks. What was the purpose of the CBT? Why did you want to lose weight at that point? What was the mindset driving you there?

Nicole: ... I can't really remember. I just remember knowing that, 'I've got this problem, I need to sort it out ... nothing I'm doing at that moment is working. I'm not getting that shift. Maybe I'll try this.'

Windy: So like a problem-oriented mindset: 'I've got a problem, I need to sort it out.'

Nicole: Yeah.

Windy: What about the group work?

Nicole: Yeah. So there's a counsellor who focuses on binge-eating, overeating. She's got a lot of YouTubes and stuff. And I paid to have a group work type thing. ... [*Pause*] It was online. I think I found some of the stuff that she said useful, more – I don't know what the word is ... [*long pause*] like I could relate to what she was saying, I could understand what she was saying but it didn't shift anything in me.

Windy: Right, OK.

Nicole: I don't know if that makes sense at all. My brain's not functioning properly today.

Windy: No, I understand that. So why have you put it as one of the two issues for our work together? Let's review that. Where are you on that particular issue? Why is this something that you want to focus on?

[*Too many questions!*]

Nicole: Because I'm … getting bigger and bigger. I'm the biggest that I've ever been and I feel like it's just gonna continue and continue and continue, and there's gonna be no end to it. I want to be healthy.

Windy: Why?

Nicole: … So that I can be around for my kids.

Windy: If you didn't have any kids would you still want to be healthy?

Nicole: … [*Long pause*] I don't know. I was just thinking about when we went away and … we went on a ride and … [*long pause*] it was really embarrassing because the bar wouldn't go down properly and you had to really push it into my belly. It's like is it going to stop me from … [*pause*] doing things with my kids because I'm being selfish?

Windy: You're being selfish?

Nicole: Yeah.

Windy: What do you mean you're being selfish?

Nicole: … By allowing myself to get this big, to get fat because I want a chocolate bar.

Windy: Well, OK, but how do you define selfishness?

Nicole: Doing something for you and not thinking about other people and it affects them. Like my kids, it's now affecting them because there's stuff that I wouldn't do that I would normally do.

Windy: You're a counsellor, a client comes to you, tells you the same story, you tell her that she's being selfish or you think that way, right?

Nicole: Yeah, I wouldn't say that, though.

Windy: Would you think it?

Nicole: No.

Windy: Why not?

Nicole: ... [*Pause*] Because when it's happening I'm not thinking about other people; I'm not thinking how it affects. I'm just thinking ... in the moment of ... what I want, but then that's selfish. I don't know.

Windy: Why wouldn't you think of the other person like that?

Nicole: ... I don't know. I'd have probably compassion for them. Sympathy.

Windy: Compassion?

Nicole: Yeah.

Windy: That's one of your strengths, right?

Nicole: Yeah.

Windy: Compassion for others and compassion for self or just compassion for others?

Nicole: … I think both.

Windy: OK. So you might be able to draw upon that strength in our work together to deal with this issue. And what about resilience? You mentioned that as another strength. How could that be useful to you as we look at this?

Nicole: … [*Long pause*] I don't know how it could be useful. I could think of other times when I've found something to be impossible but I've done it anyway.

Windy: OK. And also you have had success at dealing with this issue. It's been driven by fear, and then the fear goes. It's been driven by like, 'Enough's enough,' and that's motivated you. Are you interested in my take on this issue, Nicole?

              [*Having reviewed what Nicole has tried to solve the issue, I don't think we have enough to use to help Nicole deal with this issue. Thus, I ask her if she is interested in my take.*]

Nicole: Yeah. I'm interested in anything that you can give, that anyone else can give 'cos I'm lost.

Windy: Yeah. It seems to me, and I think you hinted at it, it's about looking at it like how you treat your body. I think I would make it a little bit more: it's how you treat yourself.

Nicole: Yeah.

Windy: Do you care enough about yourself to do this for you?

Nicole: ... [*Long pause*] I want to say yes but I obviously don't.

Windy: So how are you going to tackle that? From what I can see, you get off to very good starts but, because the reasons, you don't sustain them because Covid goes, the fear goes, then your partner loves you. So I'm talking about something where you say, 'I want to deal with this issue because I care about myself enough in a whole host of ways: I want to be healthy for me as well as for everybody else, I want to look good for me as well as everybody else and I want to be a certain weight for me as well as for my family.' Unless you put you at the centre of this, which I don't think you ever have, Nicole.

[*My proposed solution puts her at the heart of the issue without relying on fear as she has done previously.*]

Nicole: Yeah, probably not.

Windy: I think it's been in there, the bits of you: the attractiveness bit, the health bit – 'OK, now Covid's over I don't have to worry about that.' What do you think of that? Unless you put you and your care for yourself and your acknowledgement that you are worth caring for by you, for you, unless that is really centre stage, what do you think of that idea?

Nicole: Yeah, I like it and, thinking about it, I don't know that I've ever had the opportunity to ... put me first in my life. I was the mum to my mum rather than

my mum being my mum. I had my daughter when I
was 17, so then I was her mum.

Windy: We spoke last time about you became an adult
quickly for your kid, and you started to pay attention
and nurture the kid part of yourself. Now we're
talking about putting yourself centre stage and you
nurturing you and doing all these things that you've
done for other people for you.

Nicole: ... Yeah. When you said putting me centre stage,
that's terrifying. I don't like being ... centre stage.

Windy: Well, I'm not talking about centre stage in front of
an audience. I'm talking about centre stage where
you are the audience. Is that terrifying as well?

Nicole: ... no ... [*Pause*] I guess I need to work out what
that looks like.

Windy: What what looks like?

Nicole: Putting me first.... [*Pause*] My children are first.

Windy: Yeah. You are a mother. You are in a context. What
I'm saying is, in terms of what we're talking about
– the food issue and the overeating and the weight
loss – given the fact that you're a mother and you've
got responsibilities in that area, what is it going to
mean vis-à-vis food for Nicole to put Nicole first?

Nicole: ... [*Pause*] I don't know. I feel really stuck with
that.... I don't know if you can put it in another way.

Windy: Which bit are you stuck with?

Nicole: Can you say it again?

Windy: Yeah. Given the fact that you do have responsibilities to your kids and you are going to take care of them. It's about you taking care of yourself given the fact that you're also taking care of them. It's not them first and then you. It's you both first. So, for example, if you're doing something for them with respect to food, what are you gonna do for you?

Nicole: Put me first.

Windy: Yeah. But what is that gonna mean in terms of eating?

Nicole: ... I don't know.

Windy: Well, let's get really specific. Give me some episodes where you, in the very recent past, have, in your terms, overeaten? We'll have a look at that and what a different mindset might have made a difference to you?

Nicole: Yesterday.

Windy: OK, let's take yesterday.

Nicole: Yeah.... So yesterday evening after dinner and stuff, I didn't overeat all day, there wasn't that urge there, but then I had dinner and then I was like, 'Oh, a chocolate bar. I'll have another one. That's quite nice, I'll have another one.'

Windy: What's your goal then? What's the goal stemming from the part from the bit that we're talking about where you are gonna care for you and put you first? What goal is coming from that mindset?

Nicole: That mindset yesterday?

Windy: No, the mindset that we're talking about now. The mindset where you're gonna say, 'OK, I'm gonna bring a 'I care for myself' mindset to the issue of overeating. Given that I'm bringing that to this specific situation, what is my goal in this specific situation vis-à-vis how many chocolate bars, if any, I'm going to eat, based on the fact that I care for myself and want to bring that to the table, so to speak?'

Nicole: I don't need the chocolate. I wasn't hungry so there was no need for it and I'm not going to have it because I care for myself and I don't need to do that.

Windy: How does it feel to say that?

Nicole: … [*Long pause*] Not real.

Windy: No. Do you know why it's not real?

Nicole: … [*Long pause*] No.

Windy: How many times have you said or operated on that mindset?

Nicole: None, probably.

Windy: That's right. It's a mindset that we're creating. It's a mindset based on a stance that you've got to take towards yourself. In other words, you can either say, 'I'm worthwhile because I exist and I want to look after myself because of the fact,' or you could say, 'I'm worthwhile because I'm a mother. If I wasn't a mother, I wouldn't be worthwhile. I'm worthwhile if my partner loves me and I wouldn't be worthwhile if he doesn't love me.' So it's like this unconditional vote of confidence in you going forward – unconditional self-acceptance. What do you think of that?

Nicole: It's something that I'm willing to try. It's not a thing that I've thought about or tried before.

[I am not convinced that she is very convinced about this as a solution.]

Windy: Let's take it forward a little bit. Let's not go backwards, but coming up what are vulnerable times for you in terms of overeating here?

Nicole: ... This week I feel quite vulnerable because my partner's in America for work, so I'm here on my own with the kids. ... [Pause] And I want comfort and I'll grab food for that. And he's not here to see either.

Windy: So then bringing the mindset that we're talking about, the unconditional self-acceptance, 'I'm doing it for me because I'm important to me' mindset, how are you gonna bring that to the fore, given the fact that the reality is that you are on your own and you're feeling vulnerable? How are you gonna look after you?

Nicole: Yes.... *[Long pause]* I don't know other than reminding myself of this session and what we've spoken about.... I don't know what that looks like.

Windy: Can I do a guided imagery with you?

Nicole: Yep.

Windy: So it's tomorrow, you're on your own with the kids, they're playing and you've got the aftermath of the tinnitus. You want some comfort. You feel like a chocolate bar and then you say, 'OK, I recognise that I'm wanting some comfort. I recognise that I would usually go to a chocolate bar. I accept that. But I want to do something radically different here. I really want to deal with this because I care for myself. So that's what I'm gonna do. I'm going to care for myself. I'm going to maybe look for a different type of comfort. I don't necessarily need the comfort of a chocolate bar, although it's probably in the past the best thing for me in that respect, but, because I care for myself, I'm not gonna do that to myself or to my body or to me. I'm gonna choose a candle,' or whatever it is as an alternative. I've put that in my words and you can put it in your words, but how does that seem as a possible way forward for you?

Nicole: Yeah. It sounds good when you say it and I feel... a bit ... maybe like empowered. It feels like, when you say it like that, like I'm taking some kind of power back.

              [*Having used my words in the guided imagery, it is important that she puts it into her words.*]

Windy: Why don't you put that in your words powered by you, in your words? Again, let me set the scene. The scene is you're on your own, your partner's in the States, you're feeling a bit post-tinnitus in terms of that and you really would like the comfort of a chocolate bar. Over to you.

Nicole: ... I don't need to have a chocolate bar.... [*Pause*] I'm a powerful ... adult and ... [*pause*] I like tea, so I'm going to have a cup of tea instead. That's comforting. It's warm and it makes me feel ... warm and fuzzy. And I'm gonna take the power back because I care about me and I deserve to ... feel better.

Windy: How does that feel saying it in your own words?

Nicole: It feels better than earlier.

Windy: What I'm going to suggest is that's what you do out loud. So there's the context, the urge and the action, and in between that there's you practising this new mindset. I like the way that you generated your own alternative: 'I like tea, so I can go for tea.'

Nicole: Yeah.

Windy: So is that something that you can commit yourself to practising every time it happens?

Nicole: Yeah. I'm willing to commit to that.

Windy: Are you going to commit to that as well?

Nicole: Yes, I am.

Windy: So let's see what particularly happens, because it seems to me, just reviewing this issue, and I know that you've made several attempts on your own and in groups with CBT, etc., but I think it lacked this putting you centre stage. Putting a part of you centre stage, 'My attractiveness? Yeah, but my partner loves me. It doesn't really matter;' putting the idea, 'Oh my God, it's Covid, I'm going to have to do something to avoid getting ill. Oh, Covid's gone. I'm still here. Well, it doesn't really matter.' What it missed, where's Nicole at the centre of the stage?

Nicole: Yeah. The missing ingredient.

Windy: She cares about herself and what she puts into her body.

Nicole: Yeah.

Windy: The vital ingredient is you.

Nicole: I'm the chocolate bar.

Windy: You're the chocolate bar, yeah. I don't know what we'll call you. Nic Nac or something.

Nicole: Yeah.

Windy: I've found your Nic Nac. So do you want to summarise things and put it into your own words, as we usually do at the end of the session?

Nicole: Yeah. So the mindsets that I've had before have all been for external factors. And I'm gonna move forward with a new mindset that I'm gonna use, which is that I'm gonna put me first, me centre stage and … that's because I care about me and I'm allowing myself to do that.

Windy: Right, OK. And that's the bit between the urge and the action. Urge, new mindset, new action.

Nicole: Yeah.

Windy: But you are still going to get the urge because that's gonna come up.

Nicole: Yeah.

Windy: And it's gonna come up in a way, the association is chocolate. That's it for you.

Nicole: Yeah.

Windy: So Session 4, given the fact that we have six over six months, how much time would you like in order to put this into practice before we meet again?

Nicole: I think a few weeks.

Windy: Do you want to make an appointment now or do you wanna contact me?

Nicole: I'll contact you because I'm not sure what I'll be working, when I'll be available.

Windy: That works for you.

Nicole: Yeah.

Windy: Can I also suggest that you keep the good work going on the other issue as well.

Nicole: Yeah.

Windy: Maybe with this new insight, you could find the connection between the two as well.

Nicole: Thank you very much.

Nicole: OK, alright, take care.

[*My sense at the end of the session is that I put more energy into finding a different way for Nicole than she did. I am hoping she can capitalise on what we have done in this session enough for it to prove a solid base for the future.*]

7

Follow-up by Questionnaire and My Comments

My arrangement with Nicole was that therapy would be deemed to have finished six months after her first session with me. Consequently, on 24 January 2024 I wrote to Nicole informing her of this and sent her a follow-up questionnaire (see Appendix 4) to complete which was also part of our agreement. Nicole's completed follow-up questionnaire appears in Appendix 10. It should be noted that Nicole decided to have three sessions of the six that she could have had with me. She elaborates on this in her follow-up questionnaire.

While I want Nicole's feedback to speak for itself, I think it is necessary for me to provide some comments on our work and on her feedback, and I will do so in this chapter.

I also sent Nicole a draft of the book and invited her to comment on sections, which I have italicised here. Nicole's comments on these sections are also italicised.

Overall Progress

Nicole chose to discuss two issues with me in BTISSTM: (i) overeating and weight gain and (ii) imposter syndrome. Three months after our final session, she judged that she had made 30% progress on the former and 75% on the latter.

151

Overeating/Weight Gain

Nicole listed several issues that contributed to her progress; being supported by her partner, having stability in her life, having the time and energy to focus on this issue, joining a gym and having sessions with me. It was not clear what specific contribution our sessions made to her progress. When we focused on this issue in Session 1, my strategy was to bring to the table factors that helped her deal with this issue in the past, and her internal and external resources. In Session 3, I offered my take on the issue and encouraged Nicole to put herself more centre stage as a reason for dealing with her urges to overeat. She does make reference to this point in her follow-up questionnaire.

Nicole felt after these three sessions that BTISSTM wasn't the right approach for her to deal with this issue. I did not have the possibility of discussing this point with her as she decided not to book further sessions with me having got more of what she wanted on her other nominated issue (the imposter syndrome). I had no way of knowing that she would decide to end therapy after the third session, and I wonder what I could have done to have the opportunity to discuss this with Nicole.[23] Whether there was anything I could have done to help her with this issue is something I would wish to have had the chance to do so. And yet, it is an important principle of both SST and BTISSTM that therapy is client-led and the client chooses how many session to have with their therapist. Consequently, I fully respect Nicole's views and decision on this point.

Nicole said in response:

'After my 3rd session with Windy, I felt stuck with the overeating issue and that Windy was doing a lot of the work, which I felt bad about. The ideas and offers of his own take on things in terms of the overeating did help,

---

[23] I make some suggestions about this in Chapter 8.

but in practice – I kept hitting a brick wall. I was concerned coming back to another session saying not much has changed. On reflection, I do wonder if some contact from Windy, asking something along the lines of, "is there anything stopping you from utilising the 6 sessions or do you feel the work is done?" may have been helpful to open up a line of communication where I could have mentioned about being worried I'm not making as much progress as I had hoped for, and the fear of letting myself/him down. This may have led to further sessions depending on Windy's response. I'm conflicted as I wonder if I am passing the responsibility of change onto Windy. Ultimately, I feel regretful that this got in the way of continuing sessions.'

I think that Nicole's comments do raise the issue concerning to what extent the therapist should make some contact with the client if the client has ceased sessions before the completion of their full complement of six or whether the client should take full responsibility for not seeking further help.

Imposter Syndrome

Nicole pointed to being supported by her partner, stability and the session we had on this issue as factors that contributed to her progress. In particular, Nicole said the following on her follow-up questionnaire: 'Windy asked me to draw a picture, I am a visual person, so this was hugely beneficial to me. I could see what was going on in black and white – in front of me. It felt like a huge breakthrough and very emotional. It is something that will stick with me forever and I can't think Windy enough for this intervention. How this helped me – I am more aware of interactions with other people and bring my adult self. Reassuring my inner child that she isn't left behind.'

In my view, this intervention made a real difference to Nicole was probably the highlight of our sessions together.

Nicole said the following in response:

'*I agree this was the highlight and the big takeaway from our sessions together. I often feel like an equal when I'm with others now, both professionally and personally. It's hard to put into words how powerful the session was for me.*'

Other Issues

Nicole did not make reference to other issues in our sessions and did not say that she made any progress on any other issues.

The Therapeutic Relationship

In commenting on our therapeutic relationship, Nicole said that she experienced my caring felt that I was attuned to what she wanted to discuss.

However, she also said that as a 'people pleaser' she had to guard against exaggerating the progress she made and was worried about me being disappointed in her and in myself. The fact that she was participating in this book may also have been a factor here. She may have wanted to be a 'good client' for the project.

In SST, there is usually no time to deal with such issues. But in BTITTSM, there is more time and one thing that I could have paid more attention to when getting feedback from Nicole was her experience of our relationship and how it may have affected our work together. I need to incorporate having discussions of this nature into my BTISSTM work and maybe using the Session Rating Scale (SRS) as devised by the developers of Feedback-Informed Treatment (e.g. Prescott, Maeschalck and Miller, 2017) is worthy of consideration here (see Appendix 11). I also discuss this issue in Chapter 8.

In response, Nicole said the following:

'*I didn't feel overly concerned with being a good client for the book/the project, but more so how I would have felt in future sessions with Windy. I had thoughts that he might become frustrated with me, and I felt stuck with the problem and that I didn't have much to offer in a future session. It's also possible that my thinking Windy would be frustrated with me is just a reflection of how I feel towards myself and the issue. I was able to be honest in the follow-up questionnaire about this – a form that felt less personal and confronting and provided some distance from Windy.*'

Nicole found it helpful that I interrupted her to refocus the session, although she did say that this brought up her feelings of doing therapy 'wrong'. I think I could have gotten feedback from Nicole about how I could have interrupted her to ensure that I did it in a way that did not evoke these feelings.

Nicole did not mention anything I did that was unhelpful to her.

Forms, Transcripts and Recordings

In BTISSTM, the client is invited to complete several forms and is provided with recordings and transcripts of all sessions. The latter two features are part of my practice of BTISSTM and I do not suggest that they are integral to this way of working with clients.

Forms

I sent Nicole a pre-therapy form before her first session with me to encourage her to think about what she wanted to address in BTISSTM. I also sent a pre-session form a few days before each session to encourage her to prepare for that conversation. While Nicole said that she found the forms useful in helping her to focus on what she wanted to discuss with me, she mentioned again her urge to please me in completing the pre-session forms by sparing my feelings or by me being disappointed in her. As discussed above, I need to consider when to investigate the possible existence of such dynamics in BTISSTM and how to explore them if they do exist (see Chapter 8).

Recordings and Transcripts

Nicole chose not to listen to audio recordings of her sessions with me of read the written transcripts as she did not think doing so would help her. She preferred to process the sessions in her own way.

How BTSSTM Compares to Other Therapies

Nicole recognised that to benefit from BTISSTM clients need to have a clear goal and agenda. She valued the power being put into her hands, finding it both empowering and scary. Empowering in that she chooses what to work on; scared that she might fail because she may not be ready.

She has had more conventional therapy before noting that more time is devoted to building a trusted relationship and encouraging openness. Nicole remarked that for BTISSTM to have a good impact, the client needs to be willing to be vulnerable at the outset and be ready and motivated to address their issue and make changes.

I will discuss some of the above issues more generally in Chapter 8.

Part 3

Reflections and Conclusions

8

BTISSTM: A Work in Progress

I mentioned in the Preface that BTISSTM can best be seen at present as very much a work in progress. In this final chapter I will reflect on this way of practising brief therapy based on my work with Nicole and other clients that I have seen in BTISSTM. In doing so, I will discuss several ways of enhancing the future development of this way of practising brief therapy.

The Major Strength of BTISSTM

My view is still that the main strength of BTISSTM is that it is informed by a single-session therapy mindset. In particular, it is client-led in the sense that the client chooses both the focus of the therapy taken as a whole and that of each session that they choose to have. They are also in charge of how many sessions they have – between one and six over a six-month period – and when they choose to have them. Some clients need some reassurance from their therapist about this that whatever they choose is perfectly OK from the therapist's perspective. Some clients, like Nicole, may be overly concerned that they might not be doing therapy correctly or that they may be displeasing their therapist, for example. In Nicole's case I did not realise this, largely because I did not ask about it. I will discuss this further below.

Single-Session Therapy (SST) is particularly for people who do not want to come to therapy for a long time and the same may be true for clients who will benefit most from BTISSTM. However, such clients need to be prepared to get down to work quickly with the therapist. As Nicole reflected, 'I guess for

BTISSTM to have a good impact, the client needs to be ready and motivated to want to make a change and be willing to be vulnerable from the start with the therapist.' I will discuss how to practise BTISSTM with clients who are not necessarily in such a stage of change below.

Future Development of BTISSTM

Using a Narrow and a Wide Lens in BTISSTM

Another of BTISSTM's strengths, in my view, is that it helps clients to identify and focus on issues that have brought them to therapy. As such, the therapist and client agree and maintain a focus in each session and work towards the client's goals for change. This may be seen as using a narrow lens in BTISSTM. However, it is also possible to take a wider lens at times in the process. Using a wider lens with Nicole, I might have tried to understand her more broadly with respect to her nominated issues by inviting her to tell me more about herself from a developmental perspective, the challenges she has faced in her life, how she responded to them and what strengths she has drawn on in meeting these challenges. Here, I might also have invited her to reflect on her relational or attachment style and how this may become manifest in therapy (see below).

In response to the above, Nicole said the following:

> *'It's possible that reflecting on my relational/attachment style would have brought to the forefront my tendency to people please to which Windy may have offered clarification about the therapeutic relationship, and that this isn't a relationship where I need be concerned about pleasing him.'*

In an online programme entitled 'Irvin Yalom and the Art of Psychotherapy' (Yalom and Yalom, 2017) excerpts from Yalom's work with Luke show very nicely how it is possible within a brief therapy contract to deal with a client's specific issue and locate this in a broader understanding of relevant aspects of the client's life. While BTISSTM will almost always adopt a narrow lens there are times when adopting a wider lens helps the client more effectively with what they have come for.

The therapist should not decide alone whether or not to adopt a wider lens with a client but discuss and decide with the client. For example, I might have asked Nicole, 'In order to deal with your struggles with your weight and with what you call "imposter syndrome" do we need to focus on these issues without understanding how they may have developed over your life, or do you think we need to spend some time on this broader understanding?'

In response to the above, Nicole said:

'Perhaps also an agreement on how much time would be spent if it was chosen to spend some time on understanding the broader context. It could be easy to get carried away on the narrative, but I guess that's where Windy's refocusing skills would come in handy!'

Identifying and Working with Here and Now Relational Issues

Nicole made the point in her follow-up questionnaire that as a 'people pleaser', she had to struggle against the tendency to please me either by overestimating how much change she had made or by sparing my feelings. I mentioned in Chapter 7, I was basically unaware of this relational dynamic as it did not seem apparent in our work together. However, it is quite feasible for a therapist to ask about such relational dynamics and how it may be impacting on BTISSTM, but the therapist can only do this if they think of it. Thus, identifying and working with here-and-now relational issues between the client and therapist needs to in be the therapist's mind and space needs to be made to ask about their possible presence in therapy. How might I do this with a client in BTISSTM? One way would be to say something like, 'Sometimes a client brings into therapy sessions a tendency to relate to the therapist in the same way as they may relate to important others in their life, may I have your permission to enquire about this as it may impact the work we are doing together?'[24] Once the client has given their permission, I would then ask, 'From your perspective, how might I best bring up this issue with you?' Such a here-and-now relational issue may impact BTISSTM in two ways. First, it may affect the client's level of openness with the therapist. The client may choose not to discuss certain important points with their therapist, or they may modify how they discuss what they choose to discuss. Second, the relational issue may itself mirror the client's nominated issue. In this latter case the therapist and client have an opportunity to work with the issue with here and now immediacy.

In summary, the therapist in BTISSTM might routinely raise the possibility with the client about the presence of such here and now relational issues and if so what influence on the work this presence has.[25]

Developing and Maintaining Meta-Therapy Communication

In this chapter, I have discussed the importance of the therapist and client being able to discuss here and now relational issues that may impact on the work they do in BTISSTM. Nicole mentioned in her follow-up questionnaire that she decided that BTISSTM was not suitable for her struggles with overeating, and I remarked that I did not have an opportunity to discuss that with her. It is important therefore for the therapist and client to be

---

[24] This can also be included as an issue to be discussed in the meta-therapy communication space that I will discuss below.
[25] See Yalom & Yalom (2024) for examples of how to do this.

able to establish a 'space' where they can discuss what is going on in BTISSTM. I call this the establishment of meta-therapy communication between therapist and client.

Once this channel of communications has been established, both the therapist and the client should feel free to refer issues to the meta-therapy 'space' whenever they want to. Doing so increases therapy efficiency since potential threats to the alliance are dealt with before they become actual threats. As might be imagined, therapists and clients who have a good bond are more able to communicate about the client's therapy than those who do not have such a good bond. Consequently, it is important for the therapist to have established a good working bond with their client before discussing meta-therapy issues. Having said this, it is efficient to establish this mode of communication as early as possible in therapy so that it becomes an integral part of therapy.

Nicole commented thus:

'I like the idea of meta-therapeutic communication and that it is an added source of information to potential barriers to progress which might otherwise be unknown/unsaid. I wonder if the therapist might lead with this to model how it works in practice.'

Here is an example of how to introduce meta-communication explicitly with a client in BTISSTM.

Therapist: *An important part of BTISSTM involves us being able to 'stand back' from the work we are doing on your issues and discuss this work. I call this 'meta-therapeutic communication' which means having a discussion about therapy and how it is proceeding. What do you think of this idea?*

Client: *That makes sense, but what kind of things might we discuss?*

Therapist:　*The type of things I usually discuss with clients concerns things that aren't going as well as we both may want them to go and what my clients finding particularly helpful or unhelpful. If we get stuck, then it is particularly helpful for us to stand back and think together about how we can get unstuck. Does that make sense?*

Client:　*Yes, it does. How does it work in practice?*

Therapist:　*We can see if there is anything either of us must discuss either at the beginning of a session or at its end. Additionally, if something comes up during a session, either of us can refer it for discussion at that time.*

Client:　*That works*

Therapist:　*Would it be useful if we have a shared phrase which indicates that one or other of us wants to discuss a meta-therapy issue during a session?*

Client:　*That would be good.*

Therapist:　*What phrase would work for you?*

Client:　*Let me see. What about, 'There is something I want to discuss'?*

Therapist:　*Sounds good. Is it OK if I use that too?*

Client:　*Fine by me.*

It will be interesting to see what difference adding 'meta-therapy communication' as a key BTISSTM principle has on the effectiveness of its practice.

As I have stressed, BTISSTM is a work in progress and no doubt as I gain more experience in using it with clients, such experience with shape my ideas about this form of brief therapy and how it can be practised.

Postscript

In returning her comments that I have included in this chapter, Nicole let me know that since I sent her a copy of the book manuscript to read and comment on, she had lost weight. I asked her to reflect on this and I think her remarks are a fitting way of ending the book as they show that change can occur after BTISSTM (or any other therapy) has finished.

'I've always looked at people of a healthy weight and imagined that they have their lives together. I've felt inferior to them, like they're real adults, and I'm still not (like with the imposter syndrome). I'm still stuck feeling like a child in an adult's world, and my weight is just another part of that feeling.

So I wonder if when reading the transcripts, I recognised the imposter syndrome and weight do overlap. It's been some time since our sessions, so I felt more disconnected from it when reading through. I had more of a bird's eye view.

You know you said about generalising – I think that is what I have done with the imposter syndrome and my weight. I bring adult me to work, with my partner's friends or people I don't know, so I can also bring adult me to the dinner table and think of the snack cupboard as the kids.

That's my theory of what might have gone on anyway! It feels about right.'

Appendix 1

Therapeutic Contract with Professor Windy Dryden: Working with Individuals in Brief Therapy

Here are the elements of my practice that you need to know and agree with before you become a client of mine.

1. In my brief therapy practice:

- You can have up to six sessions with me. You can use the sessions at any interval over a six-month period.
- You do not have to use all six sessions. You can use as many or as few as you want. However, you may feel comforted knowing that all six sessions are available to you if you need them.
- You should not be in therapy with anyone else while seeing me for brief therapy as described here.
- Therapy sessions will last *up to* 50 minutes. A session finishes when the work for the session has been done. The session length is not set by the clock.
- At the outset, I will ask you to set a goal for therapy. I will also ask you at the beginning of each session for your goal for that session.
- I will encourage you to prepare for every session.
- The emphasis in each session will be on what you can take away from the session, and I will help you to implement these takeaways in your life.
- Whenever possible, I will help you to generalise your learning from sessions to other relevant areas of your life.
- I will conduct a follow-up session with you three months after you have ended therapy sessions. This is to see how you are getting on and to get your feedback about the process of therapy.
2. We will meet either face-to-face or online by Zoom. At the moment I am only offering appointments by Zoom.
3. If we are meeting online by Zoom, I will send you a link in advance.

4. All our meetings are confidential with the exception of the following:
   a. If you are at risk to yourself and are not prepared to take steps to protect your life or well-being, I will take steps to protect you in these respects.
   b. If you pose a risk to others and are not prepared to take steps to protect them, then I will take steps to protect them from you.
   c. I am professionally mandated to report past or present incidents of child abuse that have not previously been reported.
   d. If I am formally requested to hand over my notes to the courts then I am obliged to do so.
5. I will not speak or correspond with others about you without your formal, written permission. If anybody contacts me about you and I do not have your written authority to speak or correspond with them, then I will not do so and will inform you about this.
6. I have a 48-hour cancellation policy. This means that I will charge you if you do not give me full 48-hour notice that you wish to cancel your appointment. If I do not give you full 48-hour notice if I need to cancel our appointment then you do not pay for your next session. The exception to this is if either you, I or one of our loved ones have to be hospitalised.
7. My fee is ███ per 50-minute session payable by BACS at the end of the session.
   My BACS details are as follows:

Please confirm that you agree with these conditions by signing and dating a copy of this form and returning it to me.

I have read the above and agree with the conditions stated.

Signed..

Date...

Appendix 2

Pre-Therapy Form

We have agreed to meet for up to six sessions, and you will decide to have as many or as few sessions as you need. Before we meet for the first time, I invite you to complete and return this pre-therapy form before your session with me. This will help you to prepare for the sessions that we will have so that you can get the most from them. Please return it by email attachment before our first session so I can also prepare myself.

Name:
Date:

1. What issue or issues do you want to focus on in therapy?
Be concise. In one or two sentences, get to the heart of each problem.

2. Why is the issue or issues significant?
What's at stake? How does the issue or issues this affect your life? What is the future impact if the issue or issues are not resolved?

3. What do you want to achieve on this issue or issues by the end of therapy?

4. How have you tried to deal with each issue up to this point?

169

What steps, successful or unsuccessful, have you taken so far in addressing the issue?

```
┌─────────────────────────────────────────────────────┐
│                                                     │
│                                                     │
│                                                     │
│                                                     │
└─────────────────────────────────────────────────────┘
```

5. What strengths or inner resources could you draw upon while tackling the issue or issues?
If you struggle with answering this question, think what people who know you and who are on your side would say.

```
┌─────────────────────────────────────────────────────┐
│                                                     │
│                                                     │
│                                                     │
│                                                     │
└─────────────────────────────────────────────────────┘
```

6. Who are the people in your life who can support you as you tackle the issue or issues?
Name them and say what help each can provide.

```
┌─────────────────────────────────────────────────────┐
│                                                     │
│                                                     │
│                                                     │
│                                                     │
└─────────────────────────────────────────────────────┘
```

7. If you have nominated more than one issue in your response to Question 1, which issue do you want to tackle first in therapy?
Please explain your choice.

```
┌─────────────────────────────────────────────────────┐
│                                                     │
│                                                     │
│                                                     │
│                                                     │
└─────────────────────────────────────────────────────┘
```

8. What do you want to achieve by the end of our first (and perhaps only) session?

```



```

9. List below anything you think I need to know about you that if I did not know then, from your perspective, I would not be able to help you.

```


```

Thank you.

Windy Dryden

Appendix 3

Pre-Session Form

Before you attend our next session, I invite you to complete and return this pre-session form. This will help you to review the progress you have made since our last session and to prepare for the coming session that we will have so that you can get the most from them. Please return it by email attachment before our first session so I can also prepare myself.

Name: Session No:
Date:

1. List below what you did since the last session to help yourself with the issue we discussed in that session

2. Since the last session, what progress have you made on the issue or issues you indicated that you wanted to focus on in therapy?

List each issue below separately and indicate the amount of progress you have made on it by using a 0% (no progress) – 100% (problem solved). Detail the factors that helped you to make the progress listed

Issue 1: Factors that helped me make progress:

Issue 2:

Factors that helped me make progress:

Issue 3:

Factors that helped me make progress:

List other issues below, if relevant

3. What issue do you want to focus on in the upcoming session?

If this is different to the issue(s) previously listed, clarify how it relates to one or more of these issues.

4. What do you want to achieve on this issue by the end of the session?

5. How have you tried to deal with each issue up to this point?

What steps, successful or unsuccessful, have you taken so far in addressing the issue?

6. What strengths or inner resources could you draw upon while tackling the issue?

If you struggle with answering this question, think what people who know you and who are on your side would say.

```



```

7. Who are the people in your life who can support you as you tackle the issue?

Name them and say what help each can provide.

```



```

Thank you.

Windy Dryden

Appendix 4

Brief Therapy Informed by the Single-Session Therapy Mindset (BTISSTM) Follow-up Questionnaire

Name:
Date:

Please type your responses in the spaces provided.

Question	Response
1. What progress did you make on the issues that you wanted to focus on during BTISSTM. Indicate the amount of progress you have made on each one by using a 0% (no progress) – 100% (problem solved) scale.	Issue 1: Amount of progress made: Factors that helped me make progress: Factors that were absent that could have helped me make more progress:

	Issue 2: Amount of progress made: Factors that helped me make progress: Factors that were absent that could have helped me make more progress:
2. Did you make any progress on other issues that you have that you did not bring to BTISSTM? Please elaborate.	
3. How many of the six sessions did you use? Why did you choose to use that number of sessions?	
4. How would you describe your therapy relationship with Windy Dryden?	

5. What, if anything, did Windy Dryden do during therapy that was helpful to you?	
6. What, if anything, did Windy Dryden do during therapy that was unhelpful to you?	
7. How helpful did you find the pre-therapy and pre-session forms? Please elaborate.	
8. How helpful did you find the audio-recordings of your sessions? Please elaborate.	
9. How helpful did you find the transcripts of your sessions? Please elaborate.	
10. How does BTISSTM compare with other therapies that you have had? Please elaborate.	

11. What improvements, if any, do you think need to be made to the BTISS™ framework?	
12. Please give any additional feedback that your responses to the questions above have not covered.	

Thank you very much for your cooperation.

Please send your completed form back to me at windy@windydryden.com

Windy Dryden

Appendix 5

Follow-Up Telephone Evaluation Protocol

1. Check that the client has the time to talk (i.e., approximately 20–30 minutes)? Are they able and willing to talk freely, privately and in confidence?

Client Response:

Take the client through the following questions (2–5) for each of the issues the client sought help for.

2. Read to the client verbatim their original statement of the issue. Ask: 'Do you recall that?', 'Is that accurate?'

Client Response:

3. Would you say that the issue (s) is about the same or has changed? If changed, ask them to use the following five-point scale as follows:

(1) ----------------(2----------------(3)----------------(4)----------------(5)
Much worse   About the same   Much improved

Client Response:

4. What do you think made the change (for better or worse) possible. If conditions are the same, ask 'What makes it stay the same?'

Client Response:

5. If people around you have given you feedback that you have changed, how do they think you have changed?

Client Response:

6. What do you recall was particularly helpful or unhelpful from the therapy sessions you had?

Client Response:

7. How satisfied are you with the therapy that you received? Ask the client to make their rating on the following five-point scale as follows and ask them to explain their rating.

(1) ----------------(2)----------------(3)----------------(4)----------------(5)
Very   Neither satisfied   Very
dissatisfied   nor dissatisfied   satisfied

Client Response:

8. Did you find brief therapy to be sufficient? If not, would you wish to resume therapy? Would you wish to change therapist?

Client Response:

9. If you had any recommendations for improvement in the service that you received, what would they be?

Client Response:

10. Is there anything else I have not specifically asked you that you would like me to know?

Client Response:

Thank the client for their time and participation.

Appendix 6

Contract: Contributing to the 'Brief Therapy Informed by the Single-Session Mindset' Book Project

38 Bates Street
Sheffield
South Yorkshire
S10 1NQ

Phone: +44 114 478 2601
email: help@onlinevents.co.uk

onlinevents
Learning Together Online

Contract Description

This contract describes the expectations and boundaries between Windy Dryden, Onlinevents and the volunteer on the above book project.

Windy Dryden is working with Onlinevents to publish a book on brief therapy that will include a collection of transcribed sessions with the volunteer.

Description of brief therapy informed by the single-session mindset.

- The volunteer can have up to six sessions with Windy Dryden. They can use the sessions at any interval over a six-month period. These sessions will be by Zoom.

181

- The volunteer does not have to use all six sessions. They can use as many or as few as they want. However, they may feel comforted knowing that all six sessions are available to them if they need them.
- This project is not appropriate for anyone currently in therapy, and you are requested not to begin any new therapeutic relationships until after the sessions with Windy Dryden are completed.
- If you do need to begin a new, or resume a previous, therapeutic relationship before the end of the sessions with Windy Dryden, please notify Windy Dryden immediately via email to withdraw from this project.
- Therapy sessions will last *up to* 50 minutes. A session finishes when the work for the session has been done. The session length is not set by the clock.
- At the outset, Windy Dryden will ask the volunteer to set a goal for therapy. He will also ask them at the beginning of each session for their goal for that session.
- Windy Dryden will encourage the volunteer to prepare for every session.
- The emphasis in each session will be on what the volunteer can take away from the session, and Windy Dryden will help the volunteer to implement these takeaways in their life
- Whenever possible, Windy Dryden will help the volunteer to generalise their learning from sessions to other relevant areas of their life.

This contract is an opportunity for Windy Dryden, Onlinevents, and the volunteer to formalise their agreement with a signature.

By signing this contract, the volunteer agrees to:

1. Have transcripts of their sessions with Windy Dryden included in the book entitled 'Brief Therapy Informed by the Single-Session Therapy Mindset' published by Onlinevents.
2. Choose the name by which they will be known in the book.
3. Ensure, together with Windy Dryden, that no identifying information will appear in the book.
4. Undertake to write a 1000-word reflection on their experiences of the sessions and what happened subsequently. They will be

expected to submit this to Windy Dryden three months after their final session.

It will be possible for the volunteer to withdraw from this project by providing notice to Windy Dryden in writing (via email) at any time up to three months before the publication of the book (tba). After this date, the book will go into publication, and withdrawing from the project will not be possible.

If the volunteer has any questions about the project or the contract, please contact Windy Dryden.

Signatures

_____

The volunteer

Name:
Date:
Email address:

W Dryden

Windy Dryden

_____

Signed on behalf of Onlinevents

Appendix 7

Pre-Therapy Form

We have agreed to meet for up to six sessions, and you will decide to have as many or as few sessions as you need. Before we meet for the first time, I invite you to complete and return this pre-therapy form before your session with me. This will help you to prepare for the sessions that we will have so that you can get the most from them. Please return it by email attachment before our first session so I can also prepare myself.

Name: Nicole
Date: 21/07/23

1. What issue or issues do you want to focus on in therapy?
Be concise. In one or two sentences, get to the heart of each problem.

> 1. Imposter syndrome – feeling like a child in an adult's world.
> 2. Overeating & weight gain – using food for comfort.

2. Why is the issue or issues significant?
What's at stake? How does the issue or issues affect your life? What is the future impact if the issue or issues are not resolved?

> 1. Stops me from finishing counselling studies. Stops me from setting up my PP. Fear of being seen/found out to be not good enough. Still in the same part time job I was 5 years ago with minimum wage. I fear I will never be able to have a 'proper job' and earn enough money to live more comfortably.
> 2. My health is at stake. I don't want to see people I haven't seen in a while because they will see my weight gain which is embarrassing. My fear is that I'll get bigger and bigger and have not just health complications, but mental health will be affected to because I'll isolate myself more.

3. What do you want to achieve on this issue or issues by the end of therapy?

> 1. Feel like I'm an equal when I look at other adults
> 2. Stop using food for comfort

4. How have you tried to deal with each issue up to this point?
What steps, successful or unsuccessful, have you taken so far in addressing the issue?

> 1. Personal therapy. Counselling training. I feel I understand to some degree why I feel how I do but understanding it has not changed the feeling. Doing things outside my comfort zone but still feeling out of place. I didn't however let it stop me finishing my counselling training so that's a positive, even though it was uncomfortable experience at times.
> 2. I have tried several diets. Even a no diet, diet. Therapy. CBT. Group therapy for overeaters with a specialist. I manage to stay with eating normally for a while, perhaps maximum a few months and then go back to old habits and gain weight again.

5. What strengths or inner resources could you draw upon while tackling the issue or issues?
If you struggle with answering this question, think what people who know you and who are on your side would say.

> People on my side would probably say to be compassionate and give myself the empathy I give to others (feels like this is just self-soothing and not fixing the issue)

6. Who are the people in your life who can support you as you tackle the issue or issues?
Name them and say what help each can provide.

Rob my fiancée – very supportive in anything I do. My main cheerleader and confidence boost. Always believes in me. He's a great source of support and encouragement.
Lara my sister – A good distracter when things get too much.
Fiona my friend – always willing to listen and give a different perspective and encouragement.

---

7. If you have nominated more than one issue in your response to Question 1, which issue do you want to tackle first in therapy?
Please explain your choice.

Issue 1 – imposter syndrome

---

8. What do you want to achieve by the end of our first (and perhaps only) session?

Firstly, to understand why I feel like a child in an adult world

---

9. List below anything you think I need to know about you that if I did not know then, from your perspective, I would not be able to help you.

N/A

Thank you.

Windy Dryden

Appendix 8

Pre-Session Form: Session 2

Before you attend our next session, I invite you to complete and return this pre-session form. This will help you to review the progress you have made since our last session and to prepare for the coming session that we will have so that you can get the most from them. Please return it by email attachment before our first session so I can also prepare myself.

Name: Nicole   Session No: 2
Date: 02/08/23

1. **List below what you did since the last session to help yourself with the issue we discussed in that session.**

> I saw the issue as a challenge and because it felt like a small goal, I was able to achieve it. I think talking about it and getting it down to bitesize pieces (no pun intended) was helpful.

2. **Since the last session, what progress have you made on the issue or issues you indicated that you wanted to focus on in therapy?**
   List each issue below separately and indicate the amount of progress you have made on it by using a 0% (no progress) – 100% (problem solved). Detail the factors that helped you to make the progress listed.

> Issue 1: 5%
>
> Factors that helped me make progress: setting a small goal/seeing it as a challenge.
>
> Issue 2: 0%

Factors that helped me make progress:

List other issues below, if relevant

3. **What issue do you want to focus on in the upcoming session?**
   If this is different to the issue(s) previously listed, clarify how it relates to one or more of these issues.

Imposter syndrome/overwhelm. It relates to the first problem, and I wonder if dealing with this would leak into the other problem and help fix that at the same time.

4. **What do you want to achieve on this issue by the end of the session?**

To feel good enough and learn how to deal with being busy without getting overwhelmed. To be ok with not knowing everything and not being perfect.

5. **How have you tried to deal with each issue up to this point?**
   What steps, successful or unsuccessful, have you taken so far in addressing the issue?

Personal therapy, exploring my past. CBT.
CBT helpful for anxiety that I felt and I no longer have panic attacks.
Exploring past hasn't changed how I feel about myself and my abilities.

6. **What strengths or inner resources could you draw upon while tackling the issue?**
   If you struggle with answering this question, think what people who know you and who are on your side would say.

Organisation skills (although I question this myself)
Self-care.
Compassion for myself like I do others.

---

7. **Who are the people in your life who can support you as you tackle the issue?**
   Name them and say what help each can provide.

Rob – cuddles! Encouraging words and someone to offload to
Fiona – someone who believes in me and I can talk to about what's going on

---

Thank you.

Windy Dryden

Appendix 9

Pre-Session Form: Session 3

Before you attend our next session, I invite you to complete and return this pre-session form. This will help you to review the progress you have made since our last session and to prepare for the coming session that we will have so that you can get the most from them. Please return it by email attachment before our first session so I can also prepare myself.

Name: Nicole   Session No: 3
Date: 22-08-23

3. List below what you did since the last session to help yourself with the issue we discussed in that session

Allowed myself to spend time with little me – watched kid films. Thought about what it means to me to be an adult – being a mum/working. Beside adult things I can also spend time with little me and maybe that's all she needed?

4. Since the last session, what progress have you made on the issue or issues you indicated that you wanted to focus on in therapy?
List each issue below separately and indicate the amount of progress you have made on it by using a 0% (no progress) - 100% (problem solved). Detail the factors that helped you to make the progress listed

Issue 1: Overeating and weight gain 0%

Factors that helped me make progress:

Issue 2: Imposter syndrome 70%

Factors that helped me make progress: reflecting on my work. I think perhaps I have released something in me from the last session but I'm unsure if I can put my finger on it other than what I have stated above.

List other issues below, if relevant

8. What issue do you want to focus on in the upcoming session?
If this is different to the issue(s) previously listed, clarify how it relates to one or more of these issues.

Overeating and weight gain

9. What do you want to achieve on this issue by the end of the session?

I want some kind of shift in how I relate to food and how I treat my body. I feel like my body deserves better than what I'm giving it

10. How have you tried to deal with each issue up to this point?
What steps, successful or unsuccessful, have you taken so far in addressing the issue?

Yes – all sorts. CBT, group work, diets

11. What strengths or inner resources could you draw upon while tackling the issue?

If you struggle with answering this question, think what people who know you and who are on your side would say.

> Resilience. Compassion

12. Who are the people in your life who can support you as you tackle the issue?

Name them and say what help each can provide.

> My partner

Thank you.

Windy Dryden

Appendix 10

Brief Therapy Informed by the Single-Session Therapy Mindset (BTISSTM) Follow-up Questionnaire (Nicole)

Name: Nicole
Date: 08/02/24

Please type your responses in the spaces provided.

Question	Response
1. What progress did you make on the issues that you wanted to focus on during BTISSTM. Indicate the amount of progress you have made on each one by using a 0% (no progress) – 100% (problem solved) scale.	Issue 1: Overeating and weight gain. Amount of progress made: 30% Factors that helped me make progress: *Having a supportive partner *Having stability in my life *Having time to focus my energy on this *Joining a gym *Sessions with Windy Factors that were absent that could have helped me make more progress: I'm not sure what will help me to make more progress as I still struggle with this and feel like I'm yet to make a full breakthrough. I have made some progress (more mental than physical)

	Issue 2: Imposter Syndrome Amount of progress made: 75% Factors that helped me make progress: • Having a supportive partner • Stability • A particular session with Windy Factors that were absent that could have helped me make more progress: I'm not sure…
2. Did you make any progress on other issues that you have that you did not bring to BTISSTM? Please elaborate.	No
3. How many of the six sessions did you use? Why did you choose to use that number of sessions?	3 sessions. I felt like BTISSTM wasn't the right type of therapy for my overeating and weight gain issue. I felt like I had got what I needed with the other issue and therefore didn't feel like more sessions were needed.

4. How would you describe your therapy relationship with Windy Dryden?	I felt like Windy cared about me and what I wanted to work on. I felt like he wanted to make a difference and give me something to go away with that was of value – and he did. This was both good for feeling like I can share my issue but as a people pleaser, I in turn wanted to please Windy and had to fight against being honest with progress and being dishonest with how much what we had worked on had worked. I was worried he would be disappointed in me or himself. I realise this is a me issue and although I didn't let it affect our sessions because I was aware of it and wanted to do the sessions justice, I wonder if other clients may feel this way.
5. What, if anything, did Windy Dryden do during therapy that was helpful to you?	Windy would sometimes interrupt me so that he could re-focus me/the session. This was helpful to keep the session on track although did bring up feelings of doing therapy wrong. When speaking about imposter syndrome Windy asked me to draw a picture, I am a visual person, so this was hugely beneficial to me. I could see what was going on in black and white – in front of me. It felt like a huge breakthrough and very emotional. It is something that will stick with me forever and I can't think Windy enough for this intervention. How this helped me – I am more aware of interactions with other people and bring my adult self. Reassuring my inner child that she isn't left behind. In session about the eating/weight gain it was helpful to recognise and talk

	through previous attempts to lose weight. Through that it became apparent that there was something missing. This was that I have never tried to lose weight for me. Something simple that was probably on the edge of my awareness. Although I am still struggling with this issue, I have more awareness and I feel like I know what I need to do, I just don't know how. At least I won't be wasting more time repeating the same patterns that haven't worked!
6. What, if anything, did Windy Dryden do during therapy that was unhelpful to you?	
7. How helpful did you find the pre-therapy and pre-session forms? Please elaborate.	I found the forms helpful to focus me. I understand that this is a time limited form of therapy and doing some of the work before the session seems logical. When filling in the pre therapy form for my 2nd/3rd sessions, I wanted to put that I had improved more than I had, to spare Windy's feelings or Windy being disappointed in me. This in itself is something to be explored in long term therapy. I had to push these feelings aside and focus on being honest which was difficult.

8. How helpful did you find the audio-recordings of your sessions? Please elaborate.	I didn't find them helpful as I didn't listen back to them. The idea of listening to myself being vulnerable isn't a great motivator to listening to them. I felt like I got what I needed during the sessions and allowed myself to process things in my own time. I just didn't feel the need to listen to them.
9. How helpful did you find the transcripts of your sessions? Please elaborate.	Same as above. I didn't read them although I have gone back to read a particular part of 1 session, but this was just for the benefit of filling in this feedback form.
10. How does BTISSTM compare with other therapies that you have had? Please elaborate.	There feels to be a clear goal and agenda which can be beneficial for certain issues. The pre session form handed the power to me – the client and gave me the autonomy over what to work on. This was both empowering and scary. Empowering as I provide what I want to work on, scary because I then must take responsibility and really think about my issue. It also brought up feelings of not being ready – I guess scared of failure? More conventional therapy I have had felt slower paced and time is spent is building a trusting relationship which has helped me to be more open as the sessions go on. I guess for BTISSTM to have a good impact, the client needs to be ready and motivated to want to make a change and be willing to be vulnerable from the start with the therapist.

11. What improvements, if any, do you think need to be made to the BTISSTM framework?	
12. Please give any additional feedback that your responses to the questions above have not covered.	Thank you Windy for spending time with me in sessions and for your patience. I appreciate your help and again, eternally grateful for an emotional breakthrough moment. I'm looking forward to reading the book!

Thank you very much for your cooperation.

Please send your completed form back to me at windy@windydryden.com

Windy Dryden

Appendix 11

BTISSTM Session Rating Scale

Name:
Date:

It is very important for me to monitor my therapy work. So, please rate the session you recently had with me by <u>underlining</u> the number that best fits your experience on the following scales.

The pre-session questionnaire was not useful in helping me to prepare for the session
   0 1 2 3 4 5 6 7 8 9 10
The pre-session questionnaire was useful in helping me to prepare for the session

I did not feel heard, understood or respected by Windy Dryden during our session
   0 1 2 3 4 5 6 7 8 9 10
I did feel heard, understood and respected by Windy Dryden during our session

Windy Dryden and I did not discuss what I I wanted to discuss
   0 1 2 3 4 5 6 7 8 9 10
Windy Dryden and I did discuss what I wanted to discuss

Windy Dryden's approach was not a good fit for me
   0 1 2 3 4 5 6 7 8 9 10
Windy Dryden's approach was a good fit for me

Overall, I did not get what I wanted from my session with Windy Dryden
   0 1 2 3 4 5 6 7 8 9 10
Overall, I did get what I wanted from my session with Windy Dryden

If I wanted more help, I would not choose Windy Dryden as my counsellor
   0 1 2 3 4 5 6 7 8 9 10
If I wanted more help, I would choose Windy Dryden as my counsellor

Finally, if there was anything that was particularly useful or anything I could have done to have improved the session we had, please let me know in the box below:

Thank you for your feedback. If your session was online, please email this form back to _____

References

Bor, R., Gill, S., Miller, R. & Parrott, C. (2004). *Doing Therapy Briefly.* Palgrave Macmillan.

Brown, G.S., & Jones, E.R. (2005). Implementing a feedback system in a managed care environment: What are patients teaching us? *Journal of Clinical Psychology, 61,* 187–98.

Budman, S.H., Hoyt, M.F., & Friedman, S. (eds) (1992). *The First Session in Brief Therapy.* Guilford Press.

Cannistrà, F. (2022). The single session therapy mindset: Fourteen principles gained through an analysis of the literature. *International Journal of Brief Therapy and Family Science, 12* (1), 1–26.

Dryden, W. (2022). *Single-Session Therapy: Responses to Frequently Asked Questions.* Routledge.

Elton Wilson, J. (1996). *Time-Conscious Psychological Therapy.* Routledge.

Garfield, S.L. (1998). *The Practice of Brief Psychotherapy.* 2nd edition. Wiley.

Howard, K.I., Kopta, S.M., Krause, M.S., & Orlinsky, D.E. (1986). The dose–effect relationship in psychotherapy. *American Psychologist, 41*(2), 159–64.

Hoyt, M.F. (1995). *Brief Therapy and Managed Care: Readings for Contemporary Practice.* Jossey-Bass.

Hoyt, M. F. (2018). Single-session therapy: Stories, structures, themes, cautions, and prospects. In M. F. Hoyt, M. Bobele, A. Slive, J. Young & M. Talmon (eds), *Single-Session Therapy by Walk-In or Appointment: Administrative, Clinical, and Supervisory Aspects of One-at-a-Time Services* (pp. 155–74). Routledge.

Hoyt, M. F., Rosenbaum, R. & Talmon, M. (1992). Planned single-session psychotherapy. In S. H. Budman, M. F. Hoyt & S. Friedman (eds), *The First Session in Brief Therapy* (pp. 59–86). Guilford Press.

Hoyt, M.F. & Talmon, M.F. (2014). What the literature says: An annotated bibliography. In M.F. Hoyt & M. Talmon (eds), *Capturing the Moment: Single Session Therapy and Walk-In Services* (pp. 487–516). Crown House Publishing.

Hoyt, M.F., Young, J., & Rycroft, P. (2020). Single session thinking 2020. *Australian & New Zealand Journal of Family Therapy, 41*(3), 218–30.

Koss, M. P., & Butcher, J.N. (1986). Research on brief psychotherapy. In S.L. Garfield, & A. E. Bergin (eds), *Handbook of Psychotherapy and Behavior Change: An Empirical Analysis.* 3rd edition (pp. 627–70). Wiley.

Parry, S. (2019). Introduction. In S. Parry (ed.), *The Handbook of Brief Therapies: A Practical Guide* (pp. xv–xxi). Sage Publications.

Prescott, D.S., Maeschalck, C.L., & Miller, S.D. (eds) (2017). *Feedback-Informed Treatment in Clinical Practice: Reaching for Excellence.* American Psychological Association.

Prochaska, J.O., Norcross, J.C., & DiClemente, C.C. (2007). *Changing for Good: A Revolutionary Six-Stage Program for Overcoming Bad Habits and Moving Your Life Positively Forward.* Harper Collins.

Ratner, H., George, E. & Iveson, C. (2012). *Solution-Focused Brief Therapy: 100 Key Points and Techniques.* Routledge.

Safran, J.D., & Segal, Z.V. (1990). *Interpersonal Process in Cognitive Therapy.* Basic Books.

Safran, J.D., Segal, Z.V., Vallis, T.M., Shaw, B.F., & Samstag, L.W. (1993). Assessing patient suitability for short-term cognitive therapy with an interpersonal focus. *Cognitive Therapy and Research, 17,* 23–38.

Seabury, B.A., Seabury, B.H., & Garvin, C.D. (2011). *Foundations of Interpersonal Practice in Social Work: Promoting Competence in Generalist Practice.* 3rd ed. Thousand Oaks, CA: Sage Publications.

Sifneos, P.E. (1981). Short-term anxiety-provoking psychotherapy. In S.H. Budman (ed.), *Forms of Brief Therapy* (pp. 45–81). Guilford Press.

Simon, G.E., Imel, Z.E., Ludman, E.J. & Steinfeld, B.J. (2012). Is dropout after a first psychotherapy visit always a bad outcome? *Psychiatric Services, 63* (7), 705–7.

Steenbarger, B.N. (1992). Toward science-practice integration in brief counseling and therapy. *The Counseling Psychologist, 20,* 403–50.

Steenbarger, B.N. (2002). Brief therapy. In M. Hersen & W. Sledge, *Encyclopedia of Psychotherapy.* Volume 1 (pp. 349–58). Academic Press.

Talmon, M. (1990). *Single Session Therapy: Maximising the Effect of the First (and Often Only) Therapeutic Encounter.* Jossey-Bass.

Wolberg, L.R. (1965). *Short-term Psychotherapy.* Grune & Stratton.

Yalom, I.D., & Yalom, B. (2024). *Hour of the Heart: Connecting in the Here and Now.* Piatkus.

Yalom, I.D., & Yalom, V. (2017). Yalom in session: Luke. In *Irvin Yalom and the Art of Psychotherapy. An Online Program.* Psychotherapy. Net Academy.

Young, J. (2018). SST: The misunderstood gift that keeps on giving. In M. F. Hoyt, M. Bobele, Slive, J. Young & M. Talmon (eds), *Single-Session Therapy by Walk-In or Appointment: Administrative, Clinical, and Supervisory Aspects of One-at-a-Time Services* (pp. 40–58). Routledge.

Zarbo, C., Tasca, G.A., Cattafi, F. & Compare, A. (2016). Integrative psychotherapy works. *Frontiers of Psychology, 6,* doi: 10.3389/fpsyg.2015.02021.

Index

www.ingramcontent.com/pod-product-compliance
Lightning Source LLC
Chambersburg PA
CBHW060846280326
41934CB00007B/940